C000283817

ARRANG
FUNERAL

A Book of Resources

———◆———

Fraser Smith

First published in Great Britain in 2006

Society for Promoting Christian Knowledge
36 Causton Street
London SW1P 4ST

Copyright © Fraser Smith 2006

All rights reserved. No part of this book may be reproduced or
transmitted in any form or by any means, electronic or mechanical,
including photocopying, recording, or by any information storage and
retrieval system, without permission in writing from the publisher.

SPCK does not necessarily endorse the individual views contained
in its publications.

Biblical quotations are taken from the following versions: the Good
News Bible published by the Bible Societies/HarperCollins Publishers
Ltd UK © American Bible Society, 1966, 1971, 1976, 1992, 1994; the
New King James Version, copyright © 1982 by Thomas Nelson, Inc.,
used by permission, all rights reserved; the New Revised Standard
Version of the Bible, copyright © 1989 by the Division of Christian
Education of the National Council of Churches of Christ in the USA.
Used by permission. All rights reserved. The Revised English Bible
© Oxford University Press and Cambridge University Press 1989.

British Library Cataloguing-in-Publication Data
A catalogue record for this book is available from the British Library

ISBN-13: 978–0–281–05813–6
ISBN-10: 0–281–05813–X

1 3 5 7 9 10 8 6 4 2

Typeset by Graphicraft Ltd, Hong Kong
Printed in Great Britain by BookMarque Ltd

Contents

———✦———

*To Edward and George
who taught me to look at life again
through the eyes of a child*

Introduction

In 1789 Benjamin Franklin, writing to Jean Baptiste Le Roy, famously stated that 'in this world, nothing can be said to be certain, except death and taxes'. Over two hundred years later, most of us appear to be resigned to both events, while failing to appreciate the implications. Many books are now available on every aspect of financial planning, not so many have been written on the consequences of someone dying. The fact is that, sooner or later, most of us will be required to arrange the funeral of a family member or close friend.

It is equally the case that very few of us are prepared and equipped to deal adequately with the responsibility that is thrust upon us. If you want to arrange a wedding, there are plenty of books and magazines to advise you. If you want your child to be baptized, the local vicar or minister will probably provide classes of instruction. And with both weddings and christenings you will have months, if not years, in which to make the preparations, usually in an atmosphere of joy and excitement.

When it comes to arranging a funeral, the situation is quite different. Most funerals take place within a matter of days after the death, and at a time when the person making the arrangements may be in a state of grief and shock. Many decisions will have to be made, and in a short space of time – usually within the hour that the funeral director will spend gathering the information that is required in order to arrange the funeral. Unlike baptisms and weddings, there is not the luxury of time to consider and consult with family members, to change your mind and make amendments. Most of the basic decisions taken in that initial interview with the funeral director will have been acted on within an hour or two.

Apart from all the practical considerations – what type of coffin, how many cars, what about flowers, announcements in the paper, and so on – there is also the fundamental question regarding the type of funeral that is required. Again with a baptism or wedding, most people are content with the wording of the standard service laid down in the book, and if some things don't go according to plan (the baby cries throughout, or the priest forgets the name of the bride), then it just adds to the jollity of the occasion, and provides for amusing conversation afterwards.

A funeral is a very different type of service. It is to do with painfully raw emotions – of sorrow, regret, anger, disbelief and fear. It is to commemorate the life of someone who has died, to commend them into God's hands, and to support the family and friends who are grieving. Significantly the form of service should be appropriate for the person who has died, and for their family. It may be most inappropriate to hold a formal religious service in a parish church for someone who never attended, and who didn't believe in God. Equally a funeral for a 90-year-old deeply committed Christian woman, who died peacefully in her sleep, will be very different from that of a 30-year-old man with a wife and two children who was killed tragically in a car crash. And what sort of funeral would be suitable for the family of a stillborn baby?

No one funeral service can possibly meet the needs of such widely differing situations. Sadly, many relatives are so overwhelmed by their state of grief and the complexities of arranging a funeral that they simply hand over the responsibility to the funeral director and ask him or her to deal with everything as quickly as possible. The job would no doubt be done efficiently, but the resulting service could well turn out to be cold, inappropriate, impersonal and leave the mourners feeling that their hopes and expectations had not been met. As somebody once said, 'We all die, but I only die once.' Death is a hugely important event in anybody's life. It deserves to be recognized as such for, once done, a funeral can never be repeated. Most of us would want to do the best we can in celebrating the life of, and saying goodbye to, someone we have loved for many years.

This book is written for all who are called upon to arrange a funeral. It is intended for those who have never attempted such a thing before, but who are prepared to make some effort in ensuring that the resulting service is a fitting tribute to the one who has died. It is also for those who have done it before, but who would like to do it better next time, and for those who are brave enough to arrange their own funeral, with or without consulting their family. My own father planned every aspect of his funeral and left detailed instructions, which was a great help and comfort to my sister and me at a time of deep sadness. Finally, it is offered as a resource book for the professionals – mainly clergy – for whom arranging funerals is an important aspect of their ministry.

To the clergy who read this book, I would wish to say one or two things which may not meet with general agreement, but which describe my own standpoint. The first is that, in an age when fewer and fewer people are regular attenders at public worship, there is a responsibility on the part of the minister to articulate the assurance of our faith which many members of the congregation doubt they have, but wish they had. However, this does not mean that the funeral service should be regarded as an opportunity to 'have a go at the recalcitrant sinners'. Indeed there is little in what I have written that has to do with sin, judgement and redemption. This is not to say that these doctrines do not have an important place in Christian theology, but it is to maintain that, in my opinion, a funeral service is neither the time nor the place to expound them. Consequently, the theology of these services is tilted more towards the God of compassion and grace, as revealed in Jesus, than it is towards the God who sits in judgement. For those who have little or no contact with the Church, I believe it is the merciful, loving Father who is more likely to elicit a response than the distant, disapproving Judge. Finally, in our modern, secular age, it is remarkable that people who normally never set foot inside a church nonetheless continue to turn to that church, and the Christian religion, when a loved one has died. I hope we will regard this as a practical opportunity for the Church to serve the local community as we seek to reveal the love and assurance of the risen Christ to those who have lost not just a loved one, but also hope for the future.

The suggested services are simply that – suggestions that should be adapted and personalized according to the situations and people involved. They are written not to replace, but as an alternative to, the formal funeral liturgies of the Church. The readings, prayers and music are intended as resources that can be included or excluded as desired and the addresses or homilies should all be rewritten to suit each occasion. I have simply outlined a few points for guidance in preparing words that will be both personal and relevant.

Each service follows a similar pattern or liturgy. There are five basic parts that can be described as follows.

The Gathering. The minister welcomes the mourners to the service with words that are appropriate to the occasion, recognizing that this will be a completely new experience for many. They are invited to remember with thanks the person who has died, to commend them to God, and to pray for all those who grieve.

The Word. Through prayers, readings, hymns and an address, the congregation is encouraged to think about their deceased loved one in the context of the assurance of the Christian faith. This section may include eulogies spoken by, or read on behalf of, family and friends.

The Response. Through prayers and perhaps symbolic acts (see Chapter 1) the mourners are able to express their gratitude to the one who has died, and also their own feelings of grief and loss.

The Commendation. The deceased is commended to the care of God, and the mourners are helped to say goodbye.

The Committal. This takes place as the coffin is lowered into the ground, or moved from sight in the crematorium chapel.

The material included in the book has been gathered from various sources and used by me in countless services over many years. Where possible, I have acknowledged the sources and sought permission for inclusion. To any authors whose work I have not acknowledged, I can only apologize.

Arranging and conducting a funeral service is both a huge responsibility and a great privilege – get it right, and people will always remember with gratitude. Get it wrong, and they may neither forget nor forgive.

Fraser Smith

1

Preparation and participation

———◆———

I want to begin this chapter with a word of reassurance to people who have never before had the responsibility of arranging a funeral, and who don't know where to start. Most people find that the professionals with whom they have to deal are, on the whole, most sympathetic and helpful. This will include hospital administrators, doctors, funeral directors, registrars, coroners, solicitors and clergy. They will guide you through the procedure, each one passing you on to the next person in the chain. It has to be said, however, that in some cases, the amount of work they do on your behalf will be reflected in the bill you eventually receive. The most comprehensive book written on this subject is the *Which?* Consumer Guide, *What to Do When Someone Dies* by Paul Harris. As well as good bookshops, many public libraries also keep a copy.

As far as the funeral service itself is concerned, the first thing to do is to choose a good funeral director. If you are uncertain, then ask someone to recommend one. Most reputable firms belong to either the Funeral Standards Council (FSC) or the National Association of Funeral Directors (NAFD). Both of these associations have codes of practice which include providing information about services and prices, a written estimate of charges and a detailed funeral account. The code covers general and professional conduct and a procedure for complaints.

There is of course no obligation to employ a funeral director. It is possible to make all the arrangements yourself, though unless you have very good reasons for doing so, I would strongly recommend seeking professional help. The funeral director will assume total responsibility for organizing and supplying all that is needed for a funeral, and provide as much care as possible for grieving relatives.

Once a funeral director has been appointed, he or she will quickly make an appointment with the client to discuss all the practical aspects of the funeral, and to explain and answer questions about the procedure. These details will include items such as date and place of service, burial or cremation, obituary notices, floral tributes, disposal of ashes. All these are significant matters that need to be decided, but the most important part of the discussion should centre on the funeral service itself, for this is what really matters, this is what people remember, rather than the number of cars in the cortège or the type of coffin.

The next key appointment to make is with the person who will conduct the service. Normally this will be a member of the clergy, though it does not have to be. As only 8 per cent of the population are regular worshippers at church, most people will not have their own minister or priest to take the service. Until fairly recently, crematoria used to have a rota of duty clergy who would spend a day at the crematorium conducting the funerals of people they had never met before. It was Ken Livingstone, writing in 1988, who observed that 'most Church of England funerals are about as moving as the checkout at a supermarket!' – and, I would say, not just Church of England funerals. Fortunately this practice has now largely ceased, but it has to be said that certain members of the clergy are far more skilled at conducting funerals than are many of their colleagues. Again it is better to ask for a minister who can be recommended by a friend or the funeral director, rather than simply to opt for the local parish priest, unless he or she is known to you as one who is 'good at funerals'. What you are looking for is someone who is sincere and competent, and who is willing to discuss with you the sort of service that you want, and that you feel is appropriate.

Having found a suitable minister, the next step is to enter into discussion about the form of service. Normally the minister will phone to arrange a convenient time to meet with members of the deceased's family. This is essential, whether or not the family is known to the minister. Certain factors can have a major bearing on the nature of the service and need to be taken into account. How religious should it be? How old was the person who has died, and what are the circumstances of the death? Was it sudden, peaceful, unexpected, tragic? What name was the person known by? It may not be remotely like the name printed on the death certificate. Similarly the names of immediate family members and close friends should be noted and referred to in the service, particularly in the prayers. It may also be appropriate to mention the name of the deceased's husband, wife or partner who has died previously – but only if theirs was a close, loving relationship. It might be that they couldn't stand the sight of each other! The minister needs to know.

A vital part of the service involves celebrating the life of the person who has died. Even if that person was very well known to the minister, it's good to invite members of the family, or a close friend, to write a few lines which describe their loved one. These should paint a picture of the deceased, and so serve as a focal point for others' thoughts and memories. Such writing provides an opportunity for personal contributions to the service by family or friends. As to how it should be written, there is no set format, for this should be very much a personal reflection. Some people write a brief biography, or life history, mentioning names, dates, places and occupations. Others simply record loving and treasured memories. In one service I conducted, the four grandchildren had each written a few lines beginning, 'My favourite memory of grandpa is . . .' Those four memories painted a moving and realistic picture of a lovely old man.

Often these contributions will be read by the minister, on behalf of the family or friend. Sometimes, the author will express the desire to read the piece themselves. This is fine but not always easy. It is one thing to sit at home and imagine that you can do it, especially if you are used to speaking in public. It is a very different thing on the day, when confronted by the coffin containing the body of your loved one, plus a large congregation and, in the front row, members of your grieving family. A simple safeguard involves the person typing out what they want to say and giving a copy to the minister so that, when the time in the service arrives, and they find that emotion has got the better of them, the minister can read it on their behalf.

Participation by family members can make an enormous difference to the atmosphere and impact of the service. In years gone by, families were much more involved in the physical preparing of a body for burial. Nowadays we are grateful that most things are taken out of our hands by the funeral directors and nursing staff, though there is a price to be paid for this, not just financially but emotionally as well. Even the floral tributes are arranged by professional florists, delivered to the funeral director who then puts them in the hearse, brings them to the church or crematorium, and after the service places them on the ground outside the chapel or beside the grave. At no point does the family actually touch or offer the flowers to the person who has died. The whole procedure is extremely impersonal and detached.

It need not be so, and should not be. The funeral service offers many opportunities for family and friends to be involved, despite the necessary activities of the funeral directors and the conducting minister. The following are just some of the personal touches that I have come across in recent years:

- children and grandchildren carrying the coffin into the church or crematorium;
- the family choosing readings, poems, hymns and music;
- a granddaughter placing on the coffin a bunch of flowers freshly picked from her grandma's garden;
- a little boy placing his special toy on the coffin. In life he could never be parted from it; in death he wanted to give it to his favourite granddad;
- a young woman playing a piano solo in church, one of her deceased friend's favourite pieces;
- in one service the family issued a request not to send flowers but to bring one flower each, which was to be placed on and around the coffin at an appropriate point in the service.

Ray Simpson, in his book *Before We Say Goodbye*, movingly tells of a couple whose little girl was born with a damaged brain and who only survived for two weeks. At the thanksgiving service, the parents Mandy and Glynn read out letters which they had written to their beloved daughter. Glynn's letter included these words:

> My darling, darling daughter Eleanor, so much to say, so much to remember in two short weeks. You were such a wanted child . . .
>
> That very first night after your birth my life changed, you had captured my heart in a way I never thought possible . . .
>
> You amazed the doctors with your fight for life. I was proud to be your personal trainer. It was a great thrill to feel your strength growing as we exercised every six hours . . .
>
> It seems to me it was your mission to open people up to love . . . I had never known such a depth of love until you were

born, my precious little one, and I know that you have changed my world and the way I look at things for ever.

When we went to register your birth we were so overcome with pride as they filled in the columns with us as father and mother. That is something that cannot be taken from us and we will treasure for ever.

Darling Ellie, there are so many things I want to say, but my heart would break . . . God bless you, my beloved daughter, you carry my heart with you.

Mandy's letter to Eleanor included these words:

I so enjoyed having you inside me, I was so proud to be pregnant. Each morning when I bathed I would talk to you, even sing to you . . .

Let me tell you about your Dad. He is the kindest man I have ever met in all my life. He is caring, considerate, gentle, selfless and a man of great faith . . .

You have been given a task to carry out that no one could have guessed . . . You have brought people together . . . You healed wounds that we longed to be closed . . .

The most beautiful and painful moment of my life came when your Dad and I held you in our arms that last hour and a half. You were so very beautiful, my little one. Your Dad and I prayed and sang to you . . . Your Dad prayed for you not to be afraid but to walk to Jesus . . . We like to think of you with your tambourine, dancing and singing before the Lord.

Obviously such a personal and heart-rending contribution would release powerful emotions of grief and sadness, but this is perfectly acceptable at a funeral, for it is a sad time, and in times of sadness the normal thing is to cry. Certainly all those attending are unlikely ever to forget Eleanor's funeral, not just for the pathos of the words, but for one other reason. During little Eleanor's brief life, her mother sometimes called her 'Sweet Pea', because she was fragile, but sweet and lovely. At the end of the service, the parents handed out to each member of the congregation a packet of sweet pea seeds labelled, 'Please grow these sweet peas in your garden in memory of Eleanor . . .' What a lovely and fitting commemoration.

Often families want to give something to the congregation as a memento of the person who has died. Some funeral directors can supply personalized bookmarks, which can be given out. I recently conducted the funeral of a prison officer colleague in the establishment where I work. His widow had arranged for buckets of yellow roses (his favourite) to be delivered to the crematorium. After the service, she handed a rose to everyone who had attended, in memory of Pete.

One important factor that needs to be taken into account when preparing the service is the length of time. Services at a crematorium normally follow on every half-hour. Allowing ten minutes for entering and leaving the chapel, this means that the time allocated to each service is usually twenty minutes. If the family wants to include hymns, extra readings, eulogies and symbolic actions as suggested above, the time limit would almost certainly be exceeded. It is possible to book a double slot which would allow a service of up to fifty minutes, but the funeral director would need to know this early on, normally at the time he or she makes the booking at the crematorium. Although this would incur an extra cost, this is far better than having to omit parts of the service at the last minute. A service in church does permit greater flexibility, but the funeral director would still need to know the approximate length of the service in order to book the appropriate time of arrival at the crematorium or cemetery.

One possible solution for alleviating this problem of time, while allowing for personal contributions, is to have the commendation and committal first, followed by a service of celebration and thanksgiving at church. A friend of mine did precisely this when her mother died. She held the short service of commendation and committal at the crematorium and invited family members and a few close friends to attend. This was immediately followed by the main service at church to which everyone was invited. Because this was to be a service of thanksgiving for a long and very full life, members of Hilda's family and friends were asked to bring a symbol which represented aspects of her life. During the service these symbols were brought forward, shown to the congregation, and placed on a table at the front of the church. They included an album containing photographs of grandchildren and great-grandchildren; a mobile phone brought by a distant relative as a reminder of weekly phone conversations; a Scrabble board and a coffee mug by two friends who played together each week; a watercolour painting completed by Hilda at the age of 97; and a well-used prayer book brought by her church visitor. In all there were nearly twenty symbols of that long, rich life, which formed the focal point of the service. A number of people commented that they found it more inspiring to look at these throughout the service, rather than at a coffin. When the service was over the whole congregation were invited to the church hall for refreshments, and the table bearing the symbols was brought from the church so that people could continue to share memories and reflections.

Much of what has been written in this chapter serves as a reminder that a funeral should not be simply limited to the words written in a church prayer book. The more it can be personalized within the basic framework of the service, the more it will become a suitable remembrance of the one who has died. There is certainly room for humour, and in many instances to include some remark or anecdote that will make people smile will be quite in keeping with the celebration of a person's life, though the amount and type of humour should never be allowed to detract from the reverence and sanctity of the occasion.

The important thing is the discussion which should take place between the family and the officiating minister. Through a sharing of ideas it ought to be possible to produce a service that is honest, appropriate and a means of great comfort to all who attend. Most of all, it should be a fitting and lasting tribute to the loved one who has died, and one of which they themselves would be proud.

The minister
We're going to need the minister
To help this heavy body into the ground.

But he won't dig the hole;
others who are stronger and weaker will have to do that.
And he won't wipe his nose and his eyes;
others who are weaker and stronger will have to do that.
And he won't bake cakes or take care of the kids –
women's work. Anyway,
what would they do at a time like this
if they didn't do that?

No, we'll get the minister to come
and take care of the words.

He doesn't have to make them up,
he doesn't have to say them well,
he doesn't have to like them
so long as they agree to obey him.

We have to have the minister
so the words will know where to go.

Imagine them circling and circling
the confusing cemetery.
Imagine them roving the earth
without anywhere to rest.

Anne Stevenson

2

A basic Christian funeral

This service, as the name implies, is designed to meet the needs of the average bereaved family whose loved one has died in what might be described as fairly normal circumstances. The deceased will have been of reasonable age and death will have been as a result of natural causes. The surviving relatives will have rejected the idea of a traditional and formal service in their local church, either because they rarely, if ever, attended Sunday worship, or for other personal reasons ('We don't like the vicar'). They would describe themselves as non-churchgoing Christians and so would like a simple, Christian-based funeral service at the local crematorium.

Such a request is fairly representative of the majority of families who find themselves with the responsibility of arranging a funeral. The service I have written here is based on one of the services contained in the *Methodist Worship Book* and has clear links with many other Christian denominations. It follows the basic five-part structure outlined in the Introduction and can be modified and adapted to meet the specific requirements of each situation.

In addition to traditional prayers and Bible readings, I try to include readings from other sources, some obviously religious, others less so, bearing in mind not only the beliefs of the immediate bereaved family, but also taking into consideration the fact that the congregation will probably contain people with a wide range of beliefs and attitudes.

Most families appear happy to be invited to contribute to the preparation of the service by choosing readings, hymns and music, and a personal eulogy, composed and written by a family member or friend, usually has far greater impact than something prepared by the minister who is often only repeating what the family has said, but with less effect. It is a most natural part of the grieving process when

9

someone has died for the family to engage in times of sharing and recounting memories. All that is required for the eulogy is for one or two people to write down some of these reminiscences, which can then be read out in the service. On a practical point, if the family agrees to write something for the minister to read out, it is vital that the script should be with the minister well before the start of the service, or for it to have been properly typed. Not everybody's handwriting is as clear as they think it is!

The majority of the people who attend a funeral will have very little appreciation or understanding of what they are doing or why they have come. If asked, they would say that they have come to pay their last respects to the one who has died. In a subtle and non-patronizing way, the minister should attempt to make it clear that together the congregation has a far greater role to play. Certainly they are there to celebrate a life that has now come to an end; they are also there to express their condolences to the family and friends who are feeling a deep sense of loss and pain. The third reason, which is often not appreciated, is that they are there to commend the deceased person into the care of God, and then to seek the dignified disposal of the body. This really is the final act of love which any individual or family can offer to their dear one, and should be approached with dignity and devotion.

A basic Christian funeral

Introductory Sentences

I am the resurrection and the life [says the Lord]. Those who believe in me, even though they die, will live, and everyone who lives and believes in me will never die. (John 11.25)

Blessed are those who mourn, for they will be comforted.
(Matthew 5.4)

God so loved the world that he gave his only Son, so that everyone who believes in him may not perish but may have eternal life. (John 3.16)

The steadfast love of the LORD never ceases, his mercies never come to an end; they are new every morning.
(Lamentations 3.22–23)

In the world you will have tribulation; but be of good cheer, I have overcome the world. (John 16.33)

God is our refuge and strength, a very present help in trouble.
(Psalm 46.1)

The Gathering

We have come here today to give thanks for the life of *N*, to commend *him/her* into the hands of God, and to remember in our prayers all those who are sad.

I'd like to begin the service with these words, and as I read them, your thoughts will turn quite naturally to *N*.

You can shed tears that *she* is gone,
Or you can smile because *she* has lived.

You can close your eyes
And pray that *she*'ll come back,
Or you can open your eyes,
And see all *she*'s left.

Your heart can be empty,
Because you can't see *her*,
Or you can be full of the love you shared.

You can turn your back on tomorrow
And live yesterday,
Or you can be happy for tomorrow
Because of yesterday.

You can remember *her* and only that *she*'s gone,
Or you can cherish *her* memory and let it live on.

You can cry and close your mind,
Be empty and turn your back,

Or you can do what *she*'d want:
Smile, open your eyes, love and go on.

Author unknown

A hymn may be sung.

Let us pray.

God our comforter,
You are our refuge and strength,
a helper close at hand in times of trouble.
Help us so to hear your word
that our fear may be dispelled,
our loneliness eased,
and our hope reawakened.
May your Holy Spirit lift us above our sorrow,
to the peace and light of your constant love;
through Jesus Christ our Lord. **Amen.**

The Word

We meet in this solemn moment to worship God;
to give thanks for the life of *N*;
to commend *him/her* to God's loving and faithful care;
and to pray for all who mourn.

In the presence of death,
Christ offers us sure ground
for hope and confidence and even for joy,
because he shared our human life and death,
was raised again triumphant

and lives for evermore.
In him his people find eternal life.

Let us then hear the words of Holy Scripture,
that from them we may draw comfort and strength.

Readings

Suggested Bible readings:

Psalm 23
Psalm 130
Psalm 103.8–18
John 14.1–6, 27
Revelation 21.1–4

In addition to these readings from the Bible, I'd like to read these words, written by Joyce Grenfell and addressed to members of her family and her friends.

> If I should go before the rest of you
> Break not a flower nor inscribe a stone,
> Nor when I'm gone speak in a Sunday voice
> But be the usual selves that I have known.
> Weep if you must,
> Parting is hell,
> But life goes on,
> So sing as well.

Joyce Grenfell (1910–79)

Then these words. I have no idea who wrote them originally, but they are perhaps appropriate for an occasion such as this, and as I read them, again your thoughts will turn quite naturally to N.

> Miss me, but let me go.
> When I come to the end of the road
> And the sun has set for me,
> I want no tears in a gloom-filled room,
> Why cry for a soul set free?
>
> Miss me a little, but not too long,
> And not with your head bowed low.

Remember the love that we once shared.
Miss me, but let me go.

For this is a journey we all must take,
And all must go alone.
It's all part of the Master's plan,
A step on the road to home.

When you are lonely and sick of heart,
Go to the friends we know,
And bury your sorrows in doing good works.
Miss me, but let me go.

Author unknown

The Address

You come to a service such as this with a whole variety of different thoughts, feelings and emotions, perhaps chief of which are feelings of sorrow and sadness, and a sense of loss; for we are reminded today not so much of the sting of death, but rather of the far greater sting and pain of bereavement, and the hurt which comes to us when we lose someone we love through death. Indeed it seems as if this is part of the cost of loving, for we cannot love someone for many years without, at the same time, being deeply hurt when they are taken from us in death. Therefore to feel, and indeed to express sorrow at a time like this, is a perfectly normal and natural reaction, even for those of us who are Christians, for we are told in the Gospels that, when Jesus heard the news of the death of his friend Lazarus, 'Jesus wept'. If it was all right for Jesus to weep in the face of death, then it is certainly all right for us to weep also.

Some of you may come today with feelings of regret, when you look back and think perhaps of things that you said and did which now you wish you hadn't said and hadn't done, or, even more commonly, we tend to think of things that we didn't say and didn't do, and now we wish we had said them and had done them. Some of you may come with feelings of uncertainty and possibly even fear, for we also wonder what, if anything, lies beyond death.

All of these are very common reactions. They are the sort of feelings which most people have at a time like this, so there is nothing unusual or unnatural about them. But I would like to suggest that most of all you have come together today to give thanks to God for the life of *N*, for the privilege of having known *him/her* and having shared in *his/her* life in a whole variety of ways. And you are here now as members of *his/her* family and friends, to represent the many people who have known and loved *N* throughout the years of *his/her* life and who would wish now to be associated with you in giving thanks to God for all that *he/she* has meant to you in the past, and for all that *he/she* will go on meaning to you in the future.

Each one of you gathered together in this chapel today will have your own particular memories of *N*, and I'd like at this point in the service to read some words written by members of *N*'s family, and, as I do so, they will no doubt trigger off your own particular thoughts and memories.

[It might be that a family member or friend wishes to say a few words.]

To those thoughts and memories, each of you will be adding your own as together we come to give thanks for so many memories of *N*, which death cannot take from us.

So today we come to give thanks for *N*'s life, and for all that *he/she* has meant to so many people. We also give thanks that, for *N*, the sufferings and tribulations of this life are now over and death is now past, and we pray that as *he/she* passes through death, so *he/she* may enter into the joy and the peace and the fellowship of God's eternal kingdom, where *he/she* may be reunited with *his/her* own loved ones (*including and perhaps especially* _____), who have already gone on before *him/her*. For part of our faith is in the belief that death is not the end, it is not final, and it does not separate us for ever from those whom we love.

A popular poem attributed to Henry Van Dyke tells of a man standing on a seashore, watching a tall ship sailing out into the distance, gradually becoming fainter, till in the end it was a mere dot on the horizon. As he stood there, watching the ship, the man said to himself, 'There, she's gone.' But then it occurred to him that in fact the ship hadn't gone at all. All that had happened was that it had disappeared from his sight, and that somewhere on the other side of the ocean there would be others waiting to greet that same ship and who would take up where he left off by saying, 'Look, here she comes.'

In a similar way, you have come together today to say of one whom you love, 'There, *he/she*'s gone.' But then to remember that in fact *he/she* hasn't gone. All that has happened is that, for a time, *he/she* has disappeared from your sight, but that somewhere, on the other side, there will be other loved ones, who have already made that same journey before *him/her*, and who will take up where you leave off, by saying, 'Look, here *he/she* comes.'

So although inevitably today will be a sad day for you, when you feel deeply a sense of loss, at the same time you can take comfort in the assurance that death is not the end, it is not final, it does not separate us for ever from those whom we love, and that one day when we too make that same journey through death, there will be our own loved ones, waiting to greet us and to welcome us safe home.

The Response

Let us pray.

Let us first remain silent for few moments as in the quietness we remember *N*, giving thanks for all that *he/she* has meant to us in the past, and for that *he/she* will go on meaning to us in the future.

Loving God, in your wisdom and grace you have given to us much joy through the lives of your departed servants. We thank you for them, and for our memories of them.

Especially today we thank you for *N*.

We praise you for your goodness and mercy that followed *him/her* all the days of *his/her* life, and for *his/her* faithfulness in the tasks to which you called *him/her*.

We thank you that for *N* the sufferings and tribulations of this life are now over, and death is now past, and we pray that you will bring us, with *him/her*, to the joy of your perfect kingdom, through Jesus Christ our Lord. **Amen.**

Father, we pray for those who mourn at this time, remembering especially _____, and all the members of *N*'s family and close friends; all those for whom the loss of a loved one has left a great emptiness in their lives which this life can never fill. Grant them the comfort of

your peace, and give to them that assurance which knows there is
nothing at all, in life or in death, that can ever separate us from your
love, or indeed from those whom we love, through Jesus Christ our
Lord. **Amen.**

Just before our final hymn and prayers, one last short poem – some
verses from a poem entitled 'Farewell my friends' (see pages 38–9).

A hymn may be sung.

The Commendation

People standing.

Let us pray.

> Loving God,
> we thank you for *N*;
> for the richness of *his/her* personality,
> for the pleasure and love,
> laughter and tears, that we shared together.
> And now, in love, we commend *N* to your perfect mercy and
> wisdom,
> for in you alone we put our trust. **Amen.**

The Lord's Prayer

> **Our Father, who art in heaven,**
> **hallowed be thy name;**
> **thy kingdom come;**
> **thy will be done;**
> **on earth as it is in heaven.**
> **Give us this day our daily bread.**
> **And forgive us our trespasses,**
> **as we forgive those who trespass against us.**
> **And lead us not into temptation;**
> **but deliver us from evil.**
> **For thine is the kingdom,**
> **the power and the glory,**
> **for ever and ever.**
> **Amen.**

[*Service in church:*

The peace of God
which passes all understanding,
keep our hearts and minds
in the knowledge and love of God
and of his Son, Jesus Christ our Lord;
and the blessing of God,
the Father, the Son and the Holy Spirit,
remain with us always. **Amen.**]

The Committal

Since the earthly life of *N* has come to an end,
we commit *his/her* body
to be cremated/ to the elements/ to be buried;
earth to earth, ashes to ashes, dust to dust;
in sure and certain hope
of the resurrection to eternal life
through our Lord Jesus Christ;
to whom be glory for ever and ever. **Amen.**

I heard a voice from heaven saying: Blessed are the dead who die in the Lord; for they rest from their labours.

Father of all,
we pray for those whom we love, but see no longer.
Grant them your peace;
let light perpetual shine upon them;
and in your loving wisdom and almighty power
work in them the good purpose of your perfect will;
through Jesus Christ our Lord. **Amen.**

ECUSA Book of Common Prayer

The Blessing

And may the grace of our Lord Jesus Christ,
and the love of God,
and the comfort and fellowship of the Holy Spirit,
be with you and with those whom you love,
and with those who love you,
this day and always. **Amen.**

3

For a baby or child

In many poor countries throughout the world, where life expectancy is low, many babies die before, during or soon after birth. In more affluent countries such as our own, babies are not expected to die, and indeed the vast majority of babies are born without any complications and go on to become healthy children and adults. However, even in this country, one couple in five hundred loses a baby during pregnancy or shortly after birth. Added to this, a significant number of children die from illness and disease or from accidents or, less commonly, as a result of murder or suicide.

Nothing can prepare parents for the harrowing ordeal of learning that their baby or child has died, and research indicates that mourning often lasts longer among bereaved parents than it does among widows or widowers. When a child dies, it often feels to the mother as if part of herself and her partner has died too. Frequently the mother will have begun to build a relationship with the baby long before birth and to invest it with various fantasies. In a real sense a mother will never 'get over' the death of her child, especially on the occasions of birthdays and anniversaries. The child was to have been a link with past generations and the hope for the future. The father's attachment often grows more slowly, but normally increases once the baby begins to move, and it deepens as the child starts to develop and mature.

As well as parents, grandparents and siblings also have particular needs after the death of a child. Grandparents not only have to cope with the bereavement, but also to see their own children suffer acutely. Brothers and sisters can be overlooked as attention is focused on the dead baby or child and the distraught parents. They can suffer from feelings of having been abandoned, of insecurity and even of being responsible; they may also be confused, bewildered and frightened.

At such a time, the last thing the parents may want to be concerned with is arranging a funeral. There may be the desire to let somebody else deal with it, or to get it over with as soon as possible. Such temptations should be resisted. The funeral service is one of the few things that bereaved parents can offer to their baby or child, and they should devote time and thought to discussing the details of the service with the funeral director and the minister.

Until comparatively recently, the parents of babies who died before or at birth were neither encouraged nor given the opportunity to hold a funeral or memorial service. Their experience was regarded as an unfortunate event that was best forgotten. Today the situation is very different and hospitals adopt a far more professional and sensitive approach to parents who have suffered a miscarriage or stillbirth. The holding of a simple service that recognizes the existence of the baby, however young, and the pain of the bereaved family, is now regarded as having the potential to play an important part in the healing process.

Some couples will have a deep religious faith and be part of a religious community, and this may give them much comfort and support. Some will find that what has happened to them has challenged, if not shattered, the faith they had, and this may add to their anguish. Others will have no particular beliefs at all.

All these are factors that need to be taken into account by the minister conducting the service, and he or she will have to be acutely sensitive to the emotions and feelings of the bereaved couple and their family. They should be gently encouraged to make some contribution to the service, if only by choosing a reading (suggestions can be found in Chapter 7). Some may be brave enough to write their own poem or letter to their deceased child or baby, though it might be better if the minister offers to read it on their behalf. A choice of music might also be a possibility, though the minister will need to be quite tolerant of the type of music that is requested. Balloons and cuddly toys are also common forms of church decoration at the funeral of a baby or young child, and again such requests should be met with a sympathetic response from the minister.

Not only the words of the service, but the presence of the congregation should give comfort and assurance to the family that they are not alone in their grief, and that the love and prayers of their family and friends will be with them in the days that lie ahead.

Dear friend

Go ahead and mention my child,
the one that died, you know.
Don't worry about hurting me further,
the depth of my pain doesn't show.
Don't worry about making me cry,
I'm already crying inside.
Help me to heal by releasing the tears
that I'm trying to hide.
I'm hurt when you just keep silent,
pretending he didn't exist.
I'd rather you'd mention my child,
knowing that he has been missed.
You asked me how I'm doing,
I say 'pretty good' or 'fine',
But healing is something on-going,
I feel it will take a lifetime.

Author unknown

For a baby or child

Jesus said: 'Let the children come to me: do not try to stop them; for the kingdom of God belongs to such as these.'

(Mark 10.14)

Then he took the children in his arms, placed his hands on each of them, and blessed them.　　　　　(Mark 10.16)

If you who are bad know how to give good things to your children, how much more will your Father in heaven give good things to those who ask him.　　　　　(Matthew 7.11)

Jesus said: 'It is not your heavenly Father's will that one of these little ones should be lost.'　　　　　(Matthew 18.14)

Some people only dream of angels. We held one in our arms.

We'll love you for ever, we'll like you always,
As long as we're living, our baby you'll be.

Some souls are so special, heaven can't wait.

The Gathering

Your coming here today will be one of the most difficult and traumatic events that any of you will ever have to bear. You come carrying some of the deepest pain anyone can experience. Even in lives that have known hardship before, nothing can prepare you to face the emotion and anguish that you now feel. Your minds cry out, 'Why?' and there is no answer. Your hearts are breaking and no one can take away the pain. Everything seems wrong – not how it was meant to be. All your hopes and dreams shattered in an instant, and you feel nothing but emptiness inside.

And yet you have come. Why? If you have come to hear nice easy answers to your questions, then you will be disappointed, for we are not here today to mouth religious platitudes or to seek phoney comfort. Even after such a short life, *N* deserves better than that from us. So why have we come? We have come because we had to. What has happened is so great and so awful that we cannot cope with it on our own. We need to come together to share our grief and our disbelief with one another. We also need to share what has happened to us with God. For even if we have little faith, or the faith which we did have has been shaken by the events of the past few days, deep down we know that we stand in need of a greater love and power than any of us possesses.

So we come today not asking for cheap and easy answers, but simply to rest in the arms of a God who is also weeping with us today, and who loves and cares for each one of us more deeply and passionately than we can ever understand; a God who now cradles *N* as tenderly as any mother or father or grandparent ever did; a God who comes very close to us today, and who will never let us go.

Hymn

> Lord Jesus, take this child,
> So briefly in our care,
> Into your eternal world
> To breathe its purer air.
>
> And, as you shared their grief
> Who mourned for Lazarus,
> In our own time of sudden loss,
> Comfort and strengthen us.
>
> Bless those who seek to heal
> All kinds of human pain;
> And all who do not lose their faith,
> Though mysteries remain.
>
> As praying turns to praise,
> Together we adore
> The God who wipes away our tears
> And bids us grieve no more.

> *Fred Pratt Green (1903–2000)*
> *Tune: Franconia*

Let us pray.

> Loving God
> we are lost and it is dark;
> we are hurt, but we feel nothing;

we know, but we cannot take it in.
Be a light to our footsteps,
a balm to our wounds
and lead us to your truth;
through Jesus Christ,
your dead but risen Son.
Amen.

Derek Browning

The Word

We meet in this solemn moment to worship God;
to give thanks for the gift of *N*;
to commend *him/her* to God's loving and faithful care;
and to pray for all who mourn.

In the presence of death,
Christ offers us sure ground
for hope and confidence and even for joy,
because he shared our human life and death,
was raised again triumphant
and lives for evermore.
In him his people find eternal life.

Let us then hear the words of Holy Scripture,
that from them we may draw comfort and strength.

Readings

Suggested Bible readings:

Isaiah 43.1–5a
Luke 9.46–48

On the death of a baby before birth:

A lost dream
You were here.
Am I the only one who saw you?
I saw your birth. I felt the overwhelming joy.
I touched your soft skin
And your silky hair.

I saw you take your first steps.
I heard your first word.
I felt your hugs
And your sloppy kisses.

I saw your first day of school
And your graduation.
Your first date, you prom, and your wedding . . .
I saw it all.
I even held your babies.

All in my first weeks of pregnancy.
Now they say you are gone . . .
None of this will be.

I hear people say,
'. . . at least you lost her before you got to know her.'
Like you weren't really a person yet.

But I saw you . . . I knew you . . . I will never forget you.

Author unknown

On the death of a child:

When I miss you most

When I'm making up the packed lunches for school and your yellow box
With the picture of the Muppets isn't there
– that's when I miss you.

When I'm pegging out the clothes and your favourite sweatshirt with
Mickey Mouse on is not flapping around with the others
– that's when I miss you.

When I'm setting the table for tea,
And your place is empty,
– that's when I miss you.

When the ice cream man comes round and I buy everyone their favourite
Ice cream, and I can't buy one for you,
– that's when I miss you.

When I'm sad and lonely and nothing else will do except to have
you back

> And hear you say, 'I love you mum,'
> – that's when I miss you most of all.

Marilyn Shawe

(Further readings are to be found in Chapter 7.)

The Address

You come to this service today with a whole variety of different thoughts,
feelings and emotions – sorrow, disbelief, anger, and the big questions:
'Why has this happened to us?' 'What have we done to deserve this?'
And for some of you, 'Why has God allowed this to happen to us?'

Let me say at this point that I have no satisfactory answers to these
questions and no neat theology to account for the death of a child.
The fact is that children are not meant to die, or to suffer, and it is
important for you to hold on to that. Some well-meaning people may
try to tell you differently: that *N*'s death was God's will; part of his
plan; that he intended this to happen. Don't listen to them. The poet
Wordsworth is right when he says:

> A simple child
> That lightly draws its breath
> And feels its life in every limb:
> What should it know of death?

William Wordsworth (1770–1850),
from 'We are seven'

To say that the death of a child is God's will is a lie against God and
against your beautiful child who had so much to live for.

Even if I could find words to explain what has happened to you
and your family, so that in your mind you say, 'Oh, now I understand,'
I doubt that this would do anything to dull the pain you are now feeling. A few days ago your minds were full of hopes and plans and
dreams for *N*'s future. Now those hopes and plans have gone and your
dreams have become a nightmare, and nothing I say can reverse that
process. It all seems wrong, not how it was meant to be, and because
of this your hearts are breaking – not just with grief, but with love.

And maybe this is where we begin to see a glimmer of hope. The reason that you feel the way you do is that you loved little *N* with all your heart, and the way we love is a reflection of God's love for us. Throughout the Bible there is the image of the God who loves us as a father loves his children; the God who is revealed in Jesus as the Friend of little children; the God who declares that the secret of life itself is to be found in a child.

Listen again to these verses. First, the prophet Isaiah who has this very graphic description of the life that will follow this sad and troubled world, and of the place of children within it. Notice how beautifully he expresses the natural love and care for animals which most children possess:

> Wolves and sheep will live together in peace,
>   And leopards will lie down with young goats.
> Calves and lion cubs will feed together,
>   and little children will take care of them.

(Isaiah 11.6)

And in Mark's Gospel:

> Jesus . . . said . . . 'Let the children come to me; do not try to stop them; for the kingdom of God belongs to such as these . . . And he put his arms round [the children], laid his hands on them, and blessed them. (Mark 10.14, 16)

Add to this the God who promises that death as we know it is not the end and does not separate us for ever from those we love.

It is into the care of this loving, compassionate Father God that we come today to commend little *N*. Take comfort from this, knowing that *N* is in God's arms now, sleeping against God's heart, and in the warmth of his love *he/she* will laugh and grow into the young person God always wanted *him/her* to be – whole and beautiful and free.

I cannot offer you answers and explanations to account for what has happened to you, and even if I could I doubt that this would take away your pain. What I can offer is the love of One who will never leave you; who will allow you to weep with him and shout at him; and who will take good care of your little one, for *he/she* is part of his creation and he loves everything that he has made.

Just before our prayers I'd like to read a poem.

> He stayed for such a little while
> So small, so complete, but so frail;
> He stayed for so very short a time,
> That he hardly seemed quite real.
> But he stayed for just long enough
> For you to know his touch, his warmth.
> He stayed just long enough
> To know he was really yours.
> And when you felt you were getting to know him,
> When you thought you were just making friends,
> He heard the voice of a far greater friend
> Calling him home from the struggle of living
> To play in the sunshine of heavenly fields.
> There he can run without aids and crutches,
> There he can play and sing without tears;
> There he can wait in God's tender keeping
> Until you can join him in coming years.

Author unknown

The Response

Let us pray.

Gracious and loving God, we give you thanks today for the precious gift of *N*. That though *he/she* was taken from us far too soon, yet the impact which *he/she* had upon our lives was immense. We thank you for the joy and laughter and love that *he/she* brought, and we offer to you now the pain which we feel so deeply.

We pray for *A* and *B*, *N*'s parents. Day by day, moment by moment, comfort and uphold them. Draw them closer together to support one another with understanding and patience and gentleness.

We pray for *N*'s grandparents, as they experience the double agony of the loss of their grandchild and the pain of their own children; and for *N*'s *brother(s)* and *sister(s)*, as they try to come to terms with what has happened to them and to their family.

We pray for all the members of *N*'s family and close friends. All those for whom the death of this little child has left a great emptiness in their lives, which this life can never fill. Grant to them the comfort of your peace, which comes from knowing that death is not the end, and that there is nothing in life, or in death, that can ever separate us from your love, or indeed from those whom we love, through Jesus Christ our Lord. **Amen.**

Hymn

> O Father, on your love we call,
> When sorrow overshadows all,
> And pain that feels too great to bear
> Drives from us any words for prayer;
> > Enfold in love for evermore
> > All those we love, but see no more.
>
> Our children innocent and dear
> Were strangers to a world of fear.
> Each precious life had more to give;
> In each our hopes and dreams could live.
> > Enfold in love for evermore
> > All those we love, but see no more.
>
> So brief the joy since each was born,
> So long the years in which to mourn:
> Give us compassion to sustain
> Each other in this time of pain;
> > Enfold in love for evermore
> > All those we love, but see no more.
>
> Guard us from bitterness and hate,
> And share with us grief's crushing weight;
> Help us to live from day to day
> Until, once more, we find our way;
> > Enfold in love for evermore
> > All those we love, but see no more.
>
> When dark despair is all around,
> And falling tears the only sound,
> Light one small flame of hope that still

You walk with us and always will.
Enfold in love for evermore
All those we love, but see no more.

Jean Holloway
Tune: Melita ('Eternal Father, strong to save')

Distribution of sweet peas or spring bulbs (see Chapter 1).

The Commendation and Committal

People standing.

So, Father, having given thanks for the gift of N, we now gently hand *him/her* back to you, in the assurance of your love, and we commit *his/her* body to the *elements/ground* (earth to earth, ashes to ashes, dust to dust), in sure and certain hope of the resurrection to eternal life, through our Lord Jesus Christ. Into your loving care, O God, we entrust *him/her*. Surround *him/her* with your tenderness and compassion, and welcome *him/her* into your kingdom of love, where mourning and crying and pain are ended, and where death itself is no more.

The Blessing

The hand of the Lord is gentle,
And though we cannot understand,
He comforts with his gentle hand.

The hand of the Lord is loving,
And though it seems our hope is gone,
His love brings strength to carry on.

The hand of the Lord brings healing,
And though our hearts are filled with pain,
His healing hand brings peace again.

And may the blessing of God, Father, Son and Holy Spirit, be with you and with those whom you love, and with those who love you, now and for evermore. **Amen.**

Closing music

'Can you feel the love tonight?' (from *The Lion King*), Elton John.

4

For a young person who died in tragic circumstances

———•◆•———

There are those who would say that the death of a baby or young child is the worst thing that could happen to any parent. I wonder whether the death of a young person is an even greater tragedy. Certainly its impact is more widespread. In addition to the family and friends of a baby, a young person has his or her own circle of friends, and that can be a significant number.

Added to this is the fact that a young person has had years to develop their own personality. They will have demonstrated gifts and talents and interests; they might have belonged to different groups and organizations; they will have established friendships and relationships; they might have had a career and plans for the future. For death to have occurred at a time when the future seemed to hold so much for them is a cruel blow for everyone associated with them.

Just as we in this country don't expect a baby to die, neither do we expect to lose a young person. Yet we know that it does happen, all too frequently and for all kinds of reasons: a road traffic crash, a drug overdose, cancer, suicide, or even murder or manslaughter. Whatever the causes and whatever the circumstances, the effect on those who are left is equally devastating. At least a long illness gives time to prepare and to say goodbye. A sudden, unexpected, tragic death gives no time at all.

All these factors must be taken into account when preparing the funeral service. Any unexpected death leaves many unresolved issues and an opportunity should be given in the service (perhaps in silent prayers) for people to be able to express to the one who has been taken from them something of their love and affection, together with their inevitable regrets.

Usually the funeral of a young person will attract a large number of young people. For many of them it will be the first funeral they will have attended, and for most of them the service will confront them in a very powerful way, again perhaps for the first time, with the event of death and all the issues that go with it. It comes as something of a shock to a youngster to realize that death does not just happen to old folk, but that it can, and does, happen to their own generation, with all the implications and questions that this raises.

The service should therefore attempt to confront, in a sensitive and non-aggressive way, some of the issues surrounding life and death, and the assurance which the Christian faith offers. Even for people who feel that they have no personal religious belief, they often gain great comfort by listening to someone who sincerely does hold such faith, particularly in times of tragedy. This is not an excuse for great theological and philosophical debate but the questions that undoubtedly will be in the minds of many need to be acknowledged and addressed.

For a young person who died in tragic circumstances

Introductory Sentences

Do not be afraid – I am with you!
I am your God – let nothing terrify you!
I will make you strong and help you;
I will protect you and save you.

(Isaiah 41.10)

The Lord is my light and my salvation;
I will fear no one.
The Lord protects me from all danger;
I will never be afraid.

(Psalm 27.1)

But the righteous, though they die early, will be at rest.
For old age is not honoured for length of time,
or measured by number of years.

(Wisdom of Solomon 4.7)

The Gathering

You come to this service in a state of shock and disbelief. You will be finding it hard to accept what has happened to *N* and to you who were *his/her* family and friends. But you have come to do three very important things. First, you have come to celebrate *his/her* life, and all that *he/she* has meant to you and to many people over the years. Second, you have come to offer comfort and support to members of *N*'s family and close friends in their time of grief, and to seek God's peace for your own troubled minds. And, third, you have come to commend *N* into God's loving care and compassion.

A hymn may be sung.

Let us pray.

Loving God,
we come here today not sure what to say, or what to think.
The tragedy that ended *N*'s life
has broken our hearts as well.

With you we rejoiced in *N*'s life
 the kindness
 the laughter
 the strength.

With you we rejoiced in what *he/she* had become
and all that the future held for *him/her*.

Today we grieve for a life so tragically cut short,
for possibilities that will not now be realized,
for dreams that will not come true.

Speak to us, Lord,
words of comfort and assurance,
for we have nowhere else to turn,
and no other help but you.

These prayers we ask in the name of Jesus Christ,
who also died as a young man,
but who rose to life eternal,
our Comforter and Friend. **Amen.**

The Word

Suggested Bible readings:

Wisdom of Solomon 4.7–9, 11, 13–14
1 Thessalonians 4.13–18
John 5.24–29

Norah Leney, whose daughter died at the age of 22, wrote these words, which express the grief that all parents feel at the death of their child.

Deep sobs –
That start beneath my heart
And hold my body in a grip that hurts.
The lump that swells inside my throat
Brings pain that tries to choke.
The tears that course down my cheeks –
I drop my head in my so empty hands,

> Abandoning myself to deep, dark grief,
> And know that with the passing time
> Will come relief.
> That, though the pain may stay,
> There soon will come a day
> When I can say her name and be at peace.

Similarly, Marjorie Pizer writes this lament for Glen who was killed in a motorbike accident at the age of 19.

> The splendid youth is dead and is no more
> And who shall comfort those who are left?
> Who shall comfort the mother who has lost her son?
> Who shall comfort the sisters who have lost a brother?
> Who shall comfort the friends who have lost a friend?
> And who shall comfort the father?
> There is no comfort for those who are grieving,
> For faith is not enough
> To assuage the tearing wound of sudden death.
> O let me not drown in the flood of grief
> For all young men who died before their time,
> And for this one, so newly dead.
> O let me catch the raft of life again
> And not be swept away
> Into the darkest depths of grief and loss.

Later the same author wrote this:

> I had thought that your death
> was a waste and a destruction,
> a pain of grief hardly to be endured.
> I am only beginning to learn
> that your life was a gift and a growing
> and a loving left with me.
> The desperation of death
> destroyed the existence of love,
> but the fact of death
> cannot destroy what has been given.
> I am learning to look at your life again
> instead of your death and your departing.

The Address

The size of the congregation gathered together in this *chapel/church* today is a tribute and a testimony to the love and affection in which *N* was undoubtedly held by so many people. We are here to attempt to express our comfort for *N*'s parents and close family. If numbers alone could heal, then the massive outpouring of love and support over the past few days would have wiped away every tear from their eyes.

Yet words alone cannot achieve this. Indeed, we can hardly speak to others when we don't know what to say to ourselves in the face of such tragedy. At the very least, the fact that so many have come here today may comfort each of you in the knowledge that you are not alone in your grief, and indeed there will be others not able to come who also will be thinking of you, and praying for you, at this time.

May I begin by saying something to *N*'s young friends. News of *his/her* death naturally came as a great shock to you as it did to us all. People of *N*'s age are not meant to die. Yet the fact that *N* has died serves as a reminder that this life does not go on for ever, and death does not come only to old people. It can come to any one of us, and at any time, for life is a very precious and a very fragile thing. It is therefore something to be treasured and never taken for granted. So take good care of yourselves and of each other for the sake of your own family and friends.

It also means for all of us that, as well as cherishing life, we should also cherish one another. This involves expressing now the love we have for family and friends, and healing broken and damaged relationships while there is still time.

But our thoughts today must centre not on ourselves, but on *N* and I'm going to ask *X* if *he/she* will say a few words about *N* on behalf of *his/her* family and friends. [*Or, I will read these words written by X on behalf of his/ her family and friends.*]

And to these thoughts and memories each of you will be adding your own.

The big question for us is not 'Why has this happened?' but 'How are we going to approach this tragedy?' We have two choices. Either we can curse it with the hopelessness of this world, or we can accept it with the help of God. In the world's view, *N* is now dead; *his/her* death is meaningless, *his/her* life is futile, and that's the end of it. All we are left with are memories from the past; and for some of you that will have to do.

The other view of course presumes some religious faith, but I expect that many of you have more of a faith than you realize. It is the view that measures a person's life not by its length, but by its quality. It is the view that believes that death is not the end, not final, and that it does not separate us for ever from those we love. It is the view that believes that whether we live or whether we die, we are always in God's hands and he will never let us go.

I appreciate that for some of you this will not be an easy concept to grasp. To you, can I say this? *N* died in what might be called the springtime of *his/her* life, when *he/she* was so full of life, and with so much to look forward to. At the end of this service, as you leave the *church/chapel*, you will find at the door a sack of spring bulbs. Please take one. It will look dead, but when you get home bury it in the ground, outside in the garden or inside in a pot. For a time nothing will happen, but in the springtime it will grow into a thing of beauty and colour. Do this in remembrance of *N*.

I'd like to end with the words of a famous prayer; as I read them, I would invite you to think of *N*.

> Lord, we give our loved one back to you,
> and just as you first gave *him* to us
> and did not lose *him* in the giving,
> so we have not lost *him*
> in returning *him* to you.
> For life is eternal
> love is immortal,
> death is only an horizon,
> and an horizon is nothing
> but the limit of our earthly sight.
> We hold *him* close within our hearts,
> and there *he* shall remain,
> To walk with us throughout our lives
> Until we meet again.

William Penn (1624–91) (adapted)

The Response

Let us pray.

And let us first remain silent for a moment as, in the quietness of your minds, you simply thank God for the life of N, thanking him for all that *he/she* has meant to you in the past, and for all that *he/she* will go on meaning to you in the future.

Silence.

Gracious and loving God, we thank you today for N and for all that *he/she* has meant to us and to many people throughout the years of *his/her* life. Help us to cherish those happy memories that death cannot take from us, that they may comfort us in the future and remind us of the privilege of having shared for a time in N's life.

We thank you that for N the sufferings and tribulations of this life are now over, and death is now past, and we pray that you will bring us, with *him/her*, to the joy of your eternal kingdom.

We pray also for ourselves. The suddenness of N's death has meant that we weren't able to say all the things that we would have liked to have said. Again in a moment of silence, let us use this opportunity now to say those words – expressions of our love, and also of our regrets.

Silence.

Father, we pray for all who are sad at this time, remembering especially _____ and all the members of N's family and close friends; all those for whom the loss of a loved one has left a great emptiness in their lives which this life can never fill. Grant them that peace which comes from knowing we are all in your hands, and that you will never let us go, through Jesus Christ our Lord. **Amen**.

Just before our final [*hymn and*] prayers, one last short poem – just three verses from a poem entitled 'Farewell my friends' (see page 83 for the full poem). These words were copied by a young girl shortly before her death from cancer at the age of just 17.

> It was beautiful
> As long as it lasted,
> The journey of my life.

I have no regrets
Whatsoever, save
The pain I'll leave behind.

Farewell, farewell
My friends,
I smile and
Bid you goodbye.
No, shed no tears,
For I need them not,
All I need is your smile.

If you feel sad,
Do think of me
For that's what I'll like.
When you live in the hearts
Of those you love,
Remember then,
You never die.

Rabindranath Tagore (1861–1941)

A hymn may be sung.

The Commendation

People standing.

Let us pray.

Loving God,
We thank you for *N*.
For the richness of *his/her* personality, for the pleasure and love,
  laughter and tears, that we shared together.
And now, in love, we commend *N* to your perfect mercy and wisdom,
For in you alone we put our trust. **Amen.**

The Lord's Prayer may be said.

**Our Father, who art in heaven,
hallowed be thy name;
thy kingdom come;
thy will be done;**

on earth as it is in heaven.
Give us this day our daily bread.
And forgive us our trespasses,
as we forgive those who trespass against us.
And lead us not into temptation;
but deliver us from evil.
For thine is the kingdom,
the power and the glory,
for ever and ever.
Amen.

[Service in church:

> *The peace of God*
> *which passes all understanding,*
> *keep our hearts and minds*
> *in the knowledge and love of God*
> *and of his Son, Jesus Christ our Lord;*
> *and the blessing of God,*
> *the Father, the Son and the Holy Spirit,*
> *remain with us always.* **Amen.***]*

The Committal

Because we believe that in Christ death is not the end, and because we trust in God who is with us in life and in death, we now release *N* into God's safe keeping, and we commit *his/her* body to be cremated [*to the ground*], earth to earth, ashes to ashes, dust to dust.

In God's house there are many rooms: may *N* find there a home of joy and peace, and by his grace may *he/she* continue to grow into the person that God wants *him/her* to be, through Jesus Christ our Lord. **Amen.**

The Blessing

Send us forth, Lord, with a fresh understanding of life:
a desire to live life in all its fullness,
to dwell in peace and harmony with our family and friends,

and to live each day in a way that would be worthy,
should it prove to be our last.

And may the blessing of God, Father, Son and Holy Spirit, be with you and with those you love, and with those who love you, now and always. **Amen.**

Distribution of spring bulbs as the congregation leaves the chapel.

5

For someone who has committed suicide

————◆◆◆————

Apart from the death of a baby or child, the death of a family member or close friend who has deliberately chosen to end their life is one of the most harrowing and shocking of experiences. As well as killing themselves, the person who commits suicide also kills a part of everyone who is close to them. Though the emotional pain may be over for the one who has died, for family and friends it is only just beginning.

The situations leading up to the suicide may vary considerably, but the impact on others remains the same, the main one being a feeling of utter astonishment and bewilderment. Few are prepared for such an event in their life and most find it difficult to cope. No simple explanations can be given, for there is no single cause and the phenomenon crosses cultural, economic and social boundaries. Suicide occurs in all types of family – rich and poor, religious and faith-less, close and uncaring. Sometimes the causes may seem fairly apparent – an older person suffering from a painful or debilitating illness, or a teenager being bullied at school – but these so-called 'causes' do not normally result in suicide, and often it is difficult to determine the reasons and motives that lie behind such a devastating act.

Neither is it always clear whether a death is the result of suicide or accident (as, for example, in the case of a drug overdose, drowning or gun shot), and in most cases of suicide no note is left behind. All this resulting uncertainty only adds to the pain and confusion of the bereaved, and the feelings of having been abandoned or punished by someone who was thought to have been close.

Any death of a close family member or friend evokes powerful reactions and emotions, but in the case of suicide these can be greatly intensified – particularly feelings of disbelief, denial and guilt. There may be strong outbursts of anger and resentment at the person who chose death over life and who apparently preferred death to being with his or her family. In addition to the immediate family, a wide range of people will be affected by a suicide – friends, neighbours, work colleagues, fellow pupils, teachers and carers. All will be found asking questions of themselves:

- 'Was there something I could have said or done?'
- 'Did I miss the warning signs?'
- 'Should I have spent more time with them?'

In short, 'Was I in some way responsible for their death?' In most cases the answer will be no, for each person is ultimately responsible for their own actions. Occasionally, however, there may well be contributing factors – if a person or group of people were involved in bullying the person who has committed suicide, or if somebody failed to take seriously a threat that the person intended to harm themselves. The resulting feelings of guilt may prove difficult to dismiss.

It will clearly take a long time for those who were close to someone who has committed suicide to come to terms with what has happened, and to recover from the impact this death will have upon their lives. Most funeral services will take place within a matter of days after the event, when those attending will still be in a state of shock and disbelief. If the service is to have any real meaning and play a part in the healing process, then it is important for the bereaved family and the minister to give some thought to the content of the service. Fundamentally it must be appropriate to the beliefs and character of the individual who has died, while also addressing the raw emotions of all who will attend, especially those feelings of disbelief, sorrow, anger and guilt.

Obviously if the family has opted for a religious service there will be an opportunity to make reference to basic Christian tenets such as forgiveness and assurance of new life in Christ, where the pain and misery of this life are no more. If a non-religious service is the choice, then the main emphasis should be a celebration of the person's life, while at the same time acknowledging the serious event of their death and the impact that it will have upon so many.

For someone who has committed suicide

Lord, out of the depths I have called to you,
hear my cry, Lord.

(Psalm 130.1)

Darkness is not too dark for you,
and night is as light as day;
to you both dark and light are one.

(Psalm 139.12)

Jesus said, 'Come to me all who are weary and whose load is heavy, and I will give you rest.' (Matthew 11.28)

Jesus said, 'For the moment you are sad; but I shall see you again, and then you will be joyful, and no one shall rob you of your joy.' (John 16.22)

The Gathering

We have come here today to give thanks for the life of *N* and all that *he/she* has meant to us in the past, and all that *he/she* will go on meaning to us in the future. Through the shock and bewilderment that we now feel, we each remember the person that *N* was to us. We may never fully know or understand what it was that made *him/her* take *his/her* own life, and that will always be hard for us. We come also to commend *N* into God's care and to pray that *he/she* may now find that peace which *he/she* failed to find in this life. We also need to pray for ourselves and each other, that God will comfort and support us who have been so deeply affected by the events of the past few days.

A hymn may be sung.

Let us pray.

Gracious and loving God, we come before you today just as we are, for we can come in no other way. We are sad and bewildered, confused and shocked. We still find it difficult to accept what has happened, and we have so many questions to which there are no answers. We wonder if there was anything we could have done that would have prevented this awful tragedy, and sometimes we feel angry at this pointless loss of life.

Somehow speak to us in this service. Let the light of your love shine in our darkness. Fill our emptiness with your compassion, lift the burden that weighs so heavily upon us, and give us the peace and hope we need to carry on.

We ask these things in the name of Jesus Christ, our Saviour and our Friend. **Amen**.

The Word

We meet in this solemn moment to worship God;
to give thanks for the life of *N*;
to commend *him/her* to God's loving and faithful care;
and to pray for all who mourn.

In the presence of death,
Christ offers us sure ground
for hope and confidence and even for joy,
because he shared our human life and death,
was raised again triumphant
and lives for evermore.
In him, his people find eternal life.

Let us then hear the words of holy Scripture,
that from them we may draw comfort and strength.

Suggested Bible readings:

Psalm 139.1–4, 13–16
Romans 5.1–5
John 6.37–40

And then these words, which perhaps express the emotions some of you are experiencing.

I just feel so angry.
Inside I'm screaming, 'Why?'
The hurt of all those who loved,

And who loved you.
You've done this;
You never gave us a chance to help
To hold your hand,
To change your mind.
We haven't said goodbye,
Told you how much we love you.

I'm angry with me;
I feel I've let you down.
Did I say or do something –
Make you feel worse?
Should I have known?
Why didn't I realise?

You haven't let me say 'sorry'.
My anger won't go away.
If I could just understand.

Lord, help me through the anger;
Help me remember his love –
Not the moment he couldn't reach anyone.

Kathryn Smith

The Address

We have come together not simply to remember *N* and all that *he/she* has meant to us, but also to think of *A and B* and all the members of *N*'s family and close friends, and to support you as best we can with our love and our prayers. It's hard to imagine what you are going through today, for it's difficult for any of us to believe and accept what has happened. We are all in something of a state of shock.

N's death, and the circumstances that surrounded it, are beyond our comprehension. Perhaps none of you realized the extent of the stress and pressure *he/she* was under, and many of you will wonder whether you could, and should, have done more to help. I certainly don't pretend to know all the answers to the questions that fill your minds at this time, especially the question as to why *N* did what *he/she* did. What I can share with you are some of the things of which I am reasonably certain.

First, I am sure that N didn't deliberately set out to hurt and upset you by the manner of *his/her* death. There is a lot to be said for the phrase that coroners sometimes use at inquests, which says that a person took their own life 'when the balance of their mind was disturbed'. In other words they were unable to think through the consequences of their actions and the effect those actions would have upon others. The fact is that some people reach a point in their life when the pressures they are under prove more than they can bear, and they arrive at the conclusion that 'to live will be more miserable than to die' (Graham Greene, *The Comedians*).

Although it may seem to those of you who were close to N that *he/she* abandoned and rejected you, it is important for you to realize that this was not an act against you, it was simply the action of a person who was unable to think through, and come to terms with, the problems *he/she* was facing.

The second point I want to stress is that you are not to blame for N's death. At a time like this, it is natural to wonder whether, by what we said or did, or by what we didn't say or didn't do, we in some way contributed to N's death. Let me try to assure you that in the vast majority of cases where people commit suicide, at the end there is little that anyone could say or do that would prevent it from happening. When a person's mind is in such a state of turmoil, all rational thought becomes impossible. So although you may have many regrets today, you must not hold yourself to blame.

The feelings and emotions you are experiencing – of grief, shock, regret and anger – are quite common reactions. In time, and it may be quite a long time, these raw emotions will fade, and, though you will never forget what has happened, eventually life will begin to return to something like normality.

As for N, let us not dwell so much on the circumstances of *his/her* death, but rather on the qualities of *his/her* life. Don't let one single fatal act, committed at a time of great confusion and stress, distort your memory of N as the person you knew them to be. At this point in the service X is going to share a few thoughts and memories of N on behalf of *his/her* family and friends.

Sharing of thoughts and memories.

To those thoughts and memories each of you will be adding your own.

Can I end by sharing with you something of the faith that sustains me and that may help to sustain you through this difficult time? For many years the Church took a very dim view of those who committed suicide. Today, as our understanding of psychology and theology has increased, we regard those who end their own lives as more to be pitied than condemned. The Bible loves to describe God in terms of a shepherd caring for his flock. The prophet Ezekiel speaks of God in this way:

> As a shepherd goes in search of his sheep . . . so I shall go in search of my sheep and rescue them. I shall search for the lost, recover the straggler, bandage the injured, strengthen the sick, and give my flock their proper food.   (Ezekiel 34.12, 16)

Similarly, the God who is revealed in Jesus is spoken of as a tender shepherd whose main concern is to seek and to save the sheep that was lost.

So it is with great confidence that we entrust *N* into the hands of this loving, forgiving and compassionate God, knowing that he understands *N* far better that you did, and better even than *N* understood *him/herself*. We pray that, in the companionship of God's mercy, *N* may now discover that peace *he/she* was unable to find in this life. May that same peace also fill your hearts and minds at this distressing time, and in all the days that lie ahead.

The Response

Let us pray.

Let us remain silent for a moment as, in the quietness of your minds, you simply thank God for *N* and for all that *he/she* has meant to you in the past, and will go on meaning to you in the future.

Silence.

Gracious and loving God, we thank you today for *N* and for the good and happy times we spent together. Despite all the sadness of this moment, help us to cherish those memories which are so precious to us, and that death cannot take from us.

In your compassion and understanding forgive N's despair and *his/her* feelings that *he/she* had nothing to live for; forgive all the hurt *he/she* has caused to those who loved *him/her*, and forgive us if we could have done more to help.

We pray also for ourselves, for though N's pain and sufferings are now over, for us who are left, they are only just beginning. The suddenness of *his/her* death has taken us by surprise. We weren't prepared, and we had so much to say and do, and now it's too late. So now in a moment of silence we say to N the things that we wish we'd said in the past – of our love, and of our regrets.

Silence.

And so, Father, we pray for all those who mourn at this time, remembering especially _____ and all the members of N's family and close friends, for whom the loss of a loved one has left a great emptiness in their lives which this life can never fill. In their hurt, grant them your healing touch; in their confusion, your peace, and in their darkness, the light of your love. These prayers we ask in the name of Jesus, our Saviour and our Friend. **Amen.**

A hymn may be sung.

The Commendation

People standing.

Let us pray.

Loving God, in love and in confidence we commend N to your perfect mercy and wisdom, for in you alone we put our trust. We thank you that for N the sufferings and unhappiness of this life are now over, and death is now past; grant to *him/her* that peace which the world could not give, but which the world cannot take away – peace which comes from knowing that we are all in your hands, and you will never let us go, through Jesus Christ our Lord. **Amen.**

The Committal

Since the earthly life of N has now come to an end,
we commit *his/her* body
to be cremated/ to the elements/ to be buried;

earth to earth, ashes to ashes, dust to dust;
in sure and certain hope
of the resurrection to eternal life
through our Lord Jesus Christ;
to whom be glory for ever and ever. **Amen.**

I heard a voice from heaven saying: Blessed are the dead who die in the Lord; for they rest from their labours.

Father of all,
we pray for those whom we love, but see no longer.
Grant them your peace;
let light perpetual shine upon them;
and in your loving wisdom and almighty power
work in them the good purpose of your perfect will;
through Jesus Christ our Lord. **Amen.**

The Blessing

Go now in peace;
leave *N* in God's firm but gentle hands;
and may God, through the love and power of his Spirit,
comfort and support you,
and those who love you,
today and in all the days that are to come,
through Jesus Christ our Lord. **Amen.**

6

For someone who had little or no faith

Some years ago a funeral director phoned me and said, 'Mr Smith, I've got a family here to arrange a funeral and they say they want something simple and non-religious, so I thought of you!' As a Methodist minister I wasn't sure whether to be flattered or offended, but when I visited the family to talk about the service, they explained that as they didn't go to church, they wanted a non-religious service, but they would like to say the Lord's Prayer and sing 'Abide with Me'! Such a view is typical of many people in our society who, when it comes to arranging a funeral, are not quite sure what they believe. They don't attend places of worship, they don't pray, except in emergencies, but they do have a residual folk religion instilled in them from childhood, either from school or Sunday school. While admitting to not being religious, they would also assert that they weren't anti-religious either, and so the inclusion of the odd hymn or prayer would be quite acceptable.

Others are more definite, in that they are quite certain they do not believe in God, and want no trace of religion in the service. Some of these will request the services of a representative of the Humanist Society to conduct a God-less funeral (as indeed they are quite entitled to do); others will still find themselves in the care of a clergyman or -woman who is amenable enough to provide the type of service that they require.

In such instances, I always make it clear at the beginning of the service that I am a Christian minister, but that it is the request of the family that the service should be non-religious. This wide range of viewpoints makes it impossible to have one service that meets all needs, and ministers will have to be extremely adaptable, unless they simply refuse to conduct any service that falls outside their narrow religious remit.

In discussing with the family, it will be important to ascertain just how much religious content, if any, is desired. This will include prayers, biblical readings and hymns, and normally people will need guidance. Chapter 7 contains a number of suggestions for non-religious readings, and Chapter 9 has a list of popular music. It might also be useful to point out that, although the family has no church affiliation, there may well be those attending the service who do have some religious faith, and who would appreciate at least the inclusion of a prayer. In addition to the content of the service, questions should be asked about whether or not it is considered appropriate for the minister to wear clerical attire.

Even in non-churchgoing people, the death of a close family member is likely to raise issues to do with faith. Is there life after death? Will they be all right? Will I see them again? Such topics will need to be handled with sensitivity and care. It may well be that the family are seeking assurance and would welcome the minister expressing in the service something of the comfort of that faith which the family doubt they have, yet which they long to have. All these various options need to be discussed fully if the service is to be appropriate for the person who has died, and if it is to meet the needs of the family and friends.

For the family who really does want just a simple and non-religious service, there should be appropriate readings and music, and a time of reflection on the one who has died. A suitable poem could be read during the committal at the crematorium or graveside.

The following service will need to be greatly adapted according to the relevant factors of each situation.

For someone who had little or no faith

Introductory Sentences

Say not in grief that he is no more, but in thankfulness that he
was.   (Jewish advice in death)

Grief is not for ever, but love is.   (Anonymous)

I cannot ask for power to forget, but I can ask for greater
courage to remember.   (Anonymous)

The Gathering

You have come here today because you have loved *N* as (*husband,
wife, brother, friend, etc.*). All of you who knew *him/her* will appreciate that *he/she* was not a particularly religious person, and therefore
the family felt it would be inappropriate for this to take the form of a
religious service. Instead, we will spend some time quietly remembering *N* and in the quietness of your minds giving thanks for all that
he/she has meant to you and to many people throughout the years of
his/her life. We will reverently bid farewell to *his/her* body and seek to
comfort the members of *his/her* family and friends who naturally are
feeling a deep sense of loss at this time.

The Word

First, here are two readings that perhaps set the tone for this service.
As I read this first poem your thoughts will turn quite naturally to *N*.

You can shed tears that *she* is gone,
Or you can smile because *she* has lived.

You can close your eyes
And pray that *she*'ll come back,
Or you can open your eyes,
And see all *she*'s left.

Your heart can be empty,
Because you can't see *her*,
Or you can be full of the love you shared.

You can turn your back on tomorrow
And live yesterday,

Or you can be happy for tomorrow
Because of yesterday.

You can remember *her* and only that *she*'s gone,
Or you can cherish *her* memory and let it live on.

You can cry and close your mind,
Be empty and turn your back,

Or you can do what *she*'d want:
Smile, open your eyes, love and go on.

Author unknown

For a man:

Not, how did he die, but how did he live?
Not, what did he gain, but what did he give?
These are the units to measure the worth
of a man as a man, regardless of birth.
Not what was his church, nor what was his creed?
But had he befriended those really in need?
Was he ever ready, with a word of good cheer,
to bring back a smile, to banish a tear?
Not what did the sketch in the newspaper say,
but how many were sorry when he passed away?

Author unknown

For a woman:

After glow
I'd like the memory of me
to be a happy one.
I'd like to leave an after glow
of smiles when life is done.
I'd like to leave an echo
whispering softly down the ways,
of happy times and laughing times
and bright and sunny days.
I'd like the tears of those who grieve,
to dry before the sun

of happy memories
that I leave when life is done.

Author unknown

*(These two readings are both of a general nature. Further more specific
readings can be found in Chapter 7.)*

The Address

You come to a service such as this with a whole variety of different
thoughts, feelings and emotions, perhaps chief of which are feelings
of sorrow and sadness, and a sense of loss, for we are reminded today
not so much of the sting of death, but rather of the far greater sting
and pain of bereavement, and the hurt which comes to us when we
lose someone we love through death. Indeed it seems as if this is part
of the cost of loving, for we cannot love someone for many years without, at the same time, being deeply hurt when we lose them through
death. Therefore to feel, and indeed to express, sorrow at a time like
this is a perfectly normal and natural reaction.

Some of you may bring with you feelings of regret, when you look
back and think of things that you said and did which now you wish
you hadn't said and hadn't done, or, perhaps more commonly, we tend
to think of things that we didn't say and didn't do, and now we wish
we had said them and had done them. Some of you may come with
feelings of uncertainty and possibly even fear, for we wonder what, if
anything, lies beyond death.

All of these are very common reactions. They are the sort of feelings that most people have at a time like this, so there is nothing
unusual or unnatural about them. But I would like to suggest that
most of all you have come together today to give thanks for the life of
N, for the privilege of having known *him/her* and having shared in
his/her life in a whole variety of ways. And you are here now as members of *his/her* family and friends, to represent the many people who
have known and loved N throughout the years of *his/her* life and who
would wish now to be associated with you in giving thanks for all that
he/she has meant to you in the past, and for all that *he/she* will go on
meaning to you in the future.

Each one of you gathered together in this place today will have
your own particular memories of N, and I'd like at this point in the

service to read some words written by members of *N*'s family. As I do so, they will no doubt trigger off your own particular thoughts and tributes.

[It might be that a family member or friend wishes to say a few words.]

To those thoughts and memories, each of you will be adding your own as together we come to give thanks for so many memories of *N* which death cannot take from us.

If this is to be a non-religious service there is not much more that the minister can say in terms of an address. If the family is happy for some religious content, including one or two simple prayers, it might also be appropriate to include some words based on the story of 'The Cracked Pot'.

The cracked pot

A water-bearer in India had two large pots, hung on each end of a pole which he carried across his neck. One of the pots had a crack in it, and while the other pot was perfect and always delivered a full portion of water at the end of the long walk from the stream to the master's house, the cracked pot arrived only half full. For a whole two years this went on daily, with the bearer delivering only one and a half pots full of water in his master's house.

Of course the perfect pot was proud of its accomplishments, but the cracked pot was ashamed of its own imperfections, and miserable that it was able to accomplish only half of what it had been made to do. After two years of what it perceived to be a bitter failure, it spoke to the water-bearer one day by the stream.

'I am ashamed of myself, and I want to apologize to you.'

'Why?' asked the bearer. 'What are you ashamed of?'

'I have been able, for these past two years, to deliver only half my load because this crack in my side causes water to leak out all the way back to your master's house. Because of my flaws, you have to do all of this work and you don't get full value for your efforts,' the pot said.

The water-bearer felt sorry for the old cracked pot and in his compassion he said, 'As we return to the master's house, I want you to notice the beautiful flowers along the path.'

Indeed, as they went up the hill, the old cracked pot took notice of the sun warming the beautiful wild flowers on the side of the path, and this cheered it some. But at the end of the trail, it still felt bad because it had leaked out half its load, and so again it apologized to the bearer for its failure.

The bearer said to the pot, 'Did you notice that there were flowers only on your side of the path but not on the other pot's side? That's because I have always known about your flaw, and I took advantage of it. I sowed flower seeds on your side of the path, and every day when we walked back from the stream, you've watered them. For two years I have been able to pick these beautiful flowers to decorate my master's table. Without you being just the way you are, he would not have this beauty to grace his house.'

So each of us has our own unique flaws. They are part of who we are. We are all cracked pots. But even our flaws can be seen through the eyes of those who love us as expressions of love and beauty.

The Response

You are here today to celebrate the whole life of *N*, faults and all, and to give thanks for the privilege of having known *him/her*. We will now spend a few moments in silence as you quietly recall your own particular and precious memories.

Silence (or a suitable piece of reflective music could be played).

Let us also in the quietness gently remember all the members of *N*'s family and close friends, for whom the loss of a loved one has left a great emptiness in their lives, which this life can never fill.

Silence.

The Farewell

As we prepare ourselves to say farewell to *N*, part of the pain we feel is the pain of regret:

- for things we said and did, and now we wish we hadn't said and hadn't done; and, more commonly,

- for things we didn't say and didn't do, and now we wish we had;
- for wasted and spoilt moments and opportunities;
- for times when we were selfish, irritable, thoughtless and uncaring.

Now is the time to lay aside all those regrets and to remember that N would not want you to carry those burdens with you into the future.

Silence.

The other part of your grief comes from losing someone you love through death. But the pain you are now feeling is but a sign of your love. In another moment of silence, make your final farewell to N.

Silence.

The Committal

Please stand.

> Since N's life has now come to an end,
> we commit *his/her* body to the *elements/ground*,
> which is welcoming to us at the time of our death.
> Earth to earth, ashes to ashes, dust to dust.
> In the cycle of life and death the earth is replenished
> and life is eternally renewed.

Dorothy McRae-McMahon (adapted)

> Do not stand at my grave and weep.
> I am not there, I do not sleep.
> I am a thousand winds that blow.
> I am the diamond glints on snow.
> I am the sunlight on ripened grain.
> I am the gentle autumn rain.
>
> When you awaken in the morning's hush,
> I am the swift uplifting rush
> Of quiet birds in circled flight.
> I am the soft stars that shine at night.
> Do not stand at my grave and cry,
> I am not there; I did not die.

Mary Elizabeth Frye (1905–2004)

Light me a candle in the darkness
Give me your hand to guide me;
Speak to me softly in the silence
Give me your strength to calm me.
Lift up my eyes to see the dawn
Ending the long night of despair;
Convince me there is always morning
And hope, if you are there.

Help me to walk the road before me
With firm step, not faltering feet;
Show me the steep and rugged pathway
And the perils I may meet.
Assure me that you are listening
And can hear my prayer;
Light me a candle in the darkness,
And I shall know that you are there.

Rosemary Arthur

As we bid farewell to *N*, let us commit ourselves to loving and supporting those who miss *him/her* most, especially *A and B* and all the members of *N*'s family and close friends.

And now let us go into the world,
glad that we have loved,
free to weep for the one we have lost,
free to hold each other in our human frailty,
determined to live life to the full
As did *N* (*if appropriate*).

Dorothy McRae-McMahon

[*The Blessing*
And may the love and peace of God,
be with you and those whom you love,
and with those who love you,
today and always. **Amen.**]

7

Additional readings and poems

—◆•◆•◆—

For a baby or young child

A glimpse of a dream
A glimpse
Of a dream
That would never be.
A moment
Of long awaited elation,
anticipation.
My heart swells with joy,
A new life is growing within me.
I am so blessed.
So much more than I deserve.

Shock! Grief!
A roar of pain like nothing I have ever known!

And then it was over
so quickly,
almost like it never was.

I am forever changed in your absence.
In our brief time together
we shared a lifetime of love.

Oh, my sweet baby.
I am so sorry you could not stay.
You have touched a part of my heart
that no one else could,
and a part of my heart is gone with you.

If only things could have been different,
but they are not.

I now sit alone in my grief
emptier than I ever was before.

As you keep an ever-watchful eye
on your Daddy and me,
please know
that no one will ever take your place,
no one ever could.

I push on now to fill my empty self.
To get a glimpse
of the dream
that some day will be.

I love you, my sweet baby.

Author unknown

Just those few weeks
For those few weeks – I had you to myself.
And that seems too short a time
to be changed so profoundly.

In those few weeks I came to know you,
and to love you.

You came to trust me with your life.
Oh what a life I had planned for you!

Just those few weeks –

When I lost you, I lost a lifetime of
hopes, plans, dreams and aspirations.
A slice of my future simply vanished overnight.

Just those few weeks –

It wasn't enough time to convince others
how special and important you were.
How odd, a truly unique person has recently died
and no one is mourning the passing.

Just a mere few weeks –

And no 'normal' person would cry all night
over a tiny, unfinished baby,
or get depressed and withdrawn day after endless day.
No one would, so why am I?

You were just those few weeks, my little one.
You darted in and out of my life too quickly.
But it seems that's all the time you needed
to make my life so much richer,
and give me a small glimpse of eternity.

Susan Erling

His laughter was better than birds in the morning, his smile
Turned the edge of the wind; his memory
Disarms death and charms the surly grave.
Early he went to bed, too early we
Saw his light put out; yet we should not grieve
More than a little while,
For he lives in the earth around us, laughs from the sky.

C. Day Lewis (1904–72)

Empty places
The tractor still sits on the shelf in the store,
The overalls rest in a box.
No cowboy boots tossed on the floor by the bed
While the cowboy 'rides horse' in his socks.

No sleepy-soft smiles as I nurse him to sleep,
After reading just one story more.
Vroom-vrooms and putt-putts aren't heard in the house
No little boy plays on the floor.

No hammer and nails in a two-year-old's hands,
As he struggles to build like his dad.
No smashed thumb, 'please rocky me, Mommy,' he sobs,
No spankings – he'll never be bad.

Two impish eyes full of mischief and glee,
Two dirt-smudged small cheeks I can't kiss,

Two little-boy arms giving back my quick hug,
    These are some of the blessings we miss.

No boyish voice begging to go out with his dad,
    Out fishing or hunting for deer,
No tousled blonde crew-cut asleep in his bed,
    Drawing forth from my heart a love-tear.

Our new family picture is missing someone,
    And so is our home-life it seems,
Yet a small boy goes galloping all 'round the room,
    And he lives in my secret heart-dreams.

The tractor still waits on the shelf in the store,
    His little lamb silently sleeps.
An empty place echoes a little boy's name
In the memories my dreaming heart keeps.

Arlene Stamy

When life goes on
What is it, I wonder,
That we set our hope upon?
There must come a point in this
Grieving process when
The choice is in my own hands.

In dark moments
I played with the idea of death –
Listened to it
And enjoyed it as one might enjoy
The sweetness of forbidden fruit.

But I made a choice, a decision –
As impossible as it seems,
I must learn to live without my child;
For I really have no other choice.

It may take many years –
Much longer than others expect.
But a time must come when
I have to accept his death

In order to accept his life,
And accept my own as well.

Author unknown

Just as surely as my child
Walked towards eternal life.
I too must walk towards my own light,
Finding a way through this
Tunnel of darkness,
To the brightness of a new day.

And in my own time,
Learn to live again
With laughter, love and joy –
For myself, for my child,
For those still in need.

So just for this moment,
Just for this day,
I set my hope
Upon tomorrow.

Author unknown

Too soon
This was a life
that had hardly begun
no time to find
your place in the sun
no time to do
all you could have done
but we loved you enough for a lifetime.

No time to enjoy
the world and its wealth
no time to take life
down off the shelf
no time to sing
the song of yourself
though you had enough love for a lifetime.

Those who live long
endure sadness and tears
but you'll never suffer
the sorrowing years:
no betrayal, no anger,
no hatred, no fears,
just love – only love – in your lifetime.

Mary Yarnell

In the days shortly before her death, she would lie curled up in a chair, half dozing, half watching us as we lived out our lives around her. Smiling she would say, 'I'm so happy, I feel I've got arms tight round me.' Her death was the most exciting moment of my life. Deep in the almost overwhelming pain and grief of her going, I was still conscious of a great joy and triumph; joy that she had not been destroyed by her suffering, that she was still confident and reassured; joy that we were able to hand her back into and on to the greatest love of all; joy that this was not really the end. I felt a very real sense of a new birth – more painful, but as exciting as her first one seven years earlier. There was an inexplicable but unshakeable knowledge that all was indeed well.

Jane Davies, whose little girl Sarah died at the age of seven

Light

(for Ciaran)
My little man, down what centuries
of light did you travel
to reach us here,
your stay so short-lived;

in the twinkling of an eye
you were moving on,
bearing our name and a splinter
of the human cross we suffer;

flashed upon us like a beacon,
we wait in darkness for that light

to come round, knowing at heart
you shine forever for us.

Hugh O'Donnell

God's lent child

'I'll lend you for a little while
a child of mine,' God said.
'For you to love the while he lives
and mourn for when he's dead.
It may be six or seven years
or forty-two or three,
but will you, till I call him back,
take care of him for me?

He'll bring his charms to gladden you
and (should his stay be brief) –
you'll always have his memories
as a solace for your grief.
I cannot promise he will stay
since all from earth return,
but there are lessons taught below
I want this child to learn.

I've looked the whole world over
in search for teachers true,
and from the things that crowd life's lane
I have chosen you.
Now will you give him all your love
nor think the labour vain?
nor hate me when I come to take
this lent child back again?'

I fancied that I heard them say
'Dear Lord, thy will be done.
for all the joys this child will bring
the risk of grief we'll run.
We'll shelter him with tenderness
we'll love him while we may,
and for the happiness we've known
forever grateful stay.

But, should thine angels call for him
much sooner than we planned,
we'll brave the bitter grief that comes
and try to understand.'

Author unknown

The name, age and gender in this next poem can be adapted to suit a particular situation.

Little angel
God sent an angel to the earth . . .
the sweetest angel too;
and for such a tiny little thing,
she had so much to do.
She knew she did not have
much time on earth to stay,
so she did not waste a second;
she got started right away.

Her eyes were bright and sparkly,
she took in every turn.
She did not miss a single thing,
because she came to learn!
God sent her here to touch the
hearts of those he couldn't reach . . .
She taught them courage, strength and faith,
because she came to teach.

Her tiny little body
was so full of God above,
you felt it when you held her,
because *N* came to love.

In eleven short months she managed
what many never will.
When she went home to Jesus,
her purpose was fulfilled.
She learned and taught, loved and played,
she learned her lessons well.
I know he was so proud of her
when she went home to dwell.

But when I miss her oh so much
I can almost hear him say,
'Please understand, her work was done . . .
she did not come to stay.'

Author unknown

The end
It is time for me to go, mother; I am going.

When in the paling darkness of the lonely dawn
You stretch out your arms for the baby in the bed,
I shall say, 'Baby is not there!'
– mother I am going.

I shall become a delicate draught of air
And caress you; and I shall be ripples
in the water when you bathe;
and kiss you and kiss you again.

In the gusty night when the rain patters on the leaves
You will hear my whisper in your bed,
And my laughter will flash with the lightning
Through the open window into your room.

If you lie awake, thinking of your baby till late into the night,
I shall sing to you from the stars, 'Sleep, mother, sleep.'
On the straying moonbeams I shall steal over your bed,
And lie upon your bosom while you sleep.

I shall become a dream, and through the little opening
Of your eyelids I shall slip into the depths of your sleep;
And when you wake up and look round startled,
Like a twinkling firefly I shall flit out into the darkness.

When, on the great festival of *puja*,
The neighbours' children come and play about the house,
I shall melt into the music of the flute
And throb in your heart all day.

Dear auntie will come with *puja* presents and will ask,
'Where is our baby, sister?' Mother, you tell her softly,

'He is in the pupils of my eyes,
He is my body and my soul.'

Rabindranath Tagore (1861–1941)

A young person

A likely lad
He was my friend
I didn't know until he went away
How hard it is to show
Or wear your feelings on your sleeve.
It's hard even to think about him,
It's hard to grieve.

He taught me this:
I didn't know that one day,
Sitting in a room, I'd say
'This is all mad,
not how it's meant to go.
That door should swing
And in he'd come,
Smiling and laughing
Like a likely lad.'

But now I wait,
And nothing's said.
The door stays shut
And smiles and laughter dumb.

I cannot think of anything to say.
Perhaps we'll find fine words another day.
For now, this has to do.

Words are all choked up
And will not flow.
We called each other mate,
Mostly the best.
We shared some laughs,
Some anger, never hate.

Feelings, they all felt part of it,
What human beings do.

He was a likely lad,
That's all we need to know.

He's gone,
He was my friend.
It all seems wrong.

I thought we'd know each other
Till the end.

Christopher Hawes

Slow dance

Have you ever watched the kids
On a merry-go-round?
Or listened to the rain
Slapping on the ground?
Ever followed a butterfly's erratic flight?
Or gazed at the sun into the fading light?
You'd better slow down,
Don't dance so fast.
Time is short,
The music won't last.

Do you run through each day
On the fly?
When you ask, 'How are you?'
Do you hear the reply?
When the day is done,
Do you lie in your bed
With the next hundred chores
Running through your head?
You'd better slow down
Don't dance so fast.
Time is short.
The music won't last.

Ever told your child,
'We'll do it tomorrow'?
And in your haste,
Not see his sorrow?
Ever lost touch,
Let a good friendship die,
'Cause you never had time
To call and say, 'Hi'.
You'd better slow down,
Don't dance so fast.
Time is short,
The music won't last.

When you run so fast to get somewhere
You miss half the fun of getting there.
When you worry and hurry through your day,
It's like an unopened gift . . .
Thrown away.
Life is not a race,
Do take it slower.
Hear the music,
Before the song is over.

David L. Weatherford

For parents

Eden Rock

They are waiting for me somewhere behind Eden Rock:
My father, twenty-five, in the same suit
Of genuine Irish Tweed, his terrier Jack
Still two years old and trembling at his feet.

My mother, twenty-three, in a sprigged dress
Drawn at the waist, ribbon in her straw hat,
Has spread the stiff white cloth over the grass.
Her hair, the colour of wheat, takes on the light.

She pours tea from a Thermos, the milk straight
From an old H.P. Sauce bottle, a screw

Of paper for a cork; slowly sets out
The same three plates, the tin cups painted blue.

The sky whitens as if lit by three suns.
My mother shades her eyes and looks my way
Over the drifted stream. My father spins
A stone along the water. Leisurely,

They beckon to me from the other bank.
I hear them call, 'See where the stream-path is!
Crossing is not as hard as you may think.'

I had not thought that it would be like this.

Charles Causley

Resurrection

Is it true that after this life of ours we shall one day be awakened
by a terrifying clamour of trumpets?
Forgive me, God, but I shall console myself
that the beginning and resurrection of all us dead
will simply be announced by the crowing of the cock.

After that, we'll remain lying down a while . . .
The first to get up
will be Mother . . . We'll hear her
quietly laying the fire,
quietly putting the kettle on the stove
and cosily taking the teapot out of the cupboard.
We'll be home once more.

Vladimír Holan (1905–80),
translated from the Czech by George Theiner

I see you dancing, Father

No sooner downstairs after the night's rest
And in the door
Than you started to dance a step
In the middle of the kitchen floor.

And as you danced
You whistled.

You made your own music
Always in tune with yourself.

Well, nearly always, anyway.
You're buried now
In Lislaughtin Abbey
And whenever I think of you

I go back beyond the old man
Mind and body broken
To find the unbroken man.
It is the moment before the dance begins,

Your lips are enjoying themselves
Whistling an air.
Whatever happens or cannot happen
In the time I have to spare
I see you dancing, father.

Brendan Kennelly

In memory of my mother
I do not think of you lying in the wet clay
Of a Monaghan graveyard; I see
You walking down a lane among the poplars
On your way to the station, or happily

Going to second Mass on a summer Sunday –
You meet me and you say:
'Don't forget to see about the cattle – '
Among your earthiest words the angels stray.

And I think of you walking along a headland
Of green oats in June,
So full of repose, so rich with life –
And I see us meeting at the end of a town

On a fair day by accident, after
The bargains are all made and we can walk
Together through the shops and stalls and markets
Free in the oriental streets of thought.

O you are not lying in the wet clay,
For it is a harvest evening now and we
Are piling up the ricks against the moonlight
And you smile up at us – eternally.

      Patrick Kavanagh (1904–67)

Inside our dreams
Where do people go when they die?
Somewhere down below or in the sky?
'I can't be sure,' said Grandad, 'but it seems
They simply set up home inside our dreams.'

      Jeanne Willis

Coat
Sometimes I have wanted
To throw you off
Like a heavy coat.

Sometimes I have said
You would not let me
Breathe or move.

But now that I am free
To choose light clothes
Or none at all

I feel the cold
And all the time I think
How warm it used to be.

      Vicki Feaver

For husband and wife

This is what I wanted to sign off with
You know what I'm
like when I'm sick: I'd sooner
curse than cry. And people don't often
know what they're saying in the end.
Or I could die in my sleep.

So I'll say it now. Here it is.
Don't pay any attention
if I don't get it right
when it's for real. Blame that
on terror and pain
or the stuff they're shooting
into my veins. This is what I wanted to
sign off with. Bend
closer, listen, I love you.

Alden Nowlan (1933–83)

The cost of loving
My love hasn't died,
nor your love for me,
for I'll always have memories of you.

So I'll take all the pain,
all the sadness and hurt
that I feel from morn till I sleep;
for that is the price of having you close
and sharing my life while you lived.

Kathryn Smith

Tomorrows
After this day has darkened and gone
And I wake to the rest of my life
I shall think of the times and places we saw
When we were husband and wife.

And I know we shall visit those places we loved
And walk by the fields and the sea
Where you and I spent our happiest hours
And somehow you'll be there with me.

If I go through the woods to the top of the hill
Or run barefoot over the sand
I shall hear your voice in the wind, my love
And feel the touch of your hand.

And people who see me on my own
As they pass me on the track
Might wonder why, if I'm really alone,
I pause sometimes and look back.

To where the roadside trees are blurred
By the early evening mist;
I'll be waiting for you to catch up, my love,
From where you've stopped to rest.

And though people will find many ways to be kind
They will never understand
How I hear your voice in the sigh of the wind
And feel the touch of your hand.

Simon Bridges

You should be here
You should be here;
the mother of my children,
the daughter so cherished,
the lover of my life.

You should be here;
to see them when they laugh,
to smile when they smile,
to listen when they speak
and hold them when they cry.

But as they laugh
and as they talk,
I hear your voice
and see your smile,
and find in them
that you are here.

Kathryn Smith

No need
I see an empty place at the table.
Whose? Who else's? Who am I kidding?
The boat's waiting. No need for oars

or a wind. I've left the key
in the same place. You know where.
Remember me and all we did together.
Now, hold me tight. That's it. Kiss me
hard on the lips. There. Now
let me go, my dearest, let me go.
We shall not meet again in this life,
so kiss me goodbye now. Here, kiss me again.
Once more. There. That's enough.
Now my dearest, let me go.
It's time to be on the way.

Raymond Carver (1939–88)

An old person

Returning

When we have done
All the work we were sent
To earth to do,
We are allowed to shed our body,
Which imprisons our soul,
Like a cocoon encloses a future butterfly.

And when the time comes,
We can let go of it,
And we will be free of pain,
Free of fears and worries,
Free as a beautiful butterfly
Returning home to God.

Elisabeth Kübler Ross (1926–2004)

There is nothing the matter with me,
I'm as healthy as can be,
I have arthritis in both my knees,
And when I talk, I talk with a wheeze.
My pulse is weak and my blood is thin,
But I'm awfully well for the shape I'm in.

Arch supports I have for my feet,
Or I wouldn't be able to walk the street.
Sleep is denied me night after night,
But every morning I find I'm alright.
My memory's failing, my head's in a spin
But I'm awfully well for the shape I'm in.

Old age is golden, I've heard it said,
But sometimes I wonder as I get into bed.
With my ears in a drawer, my teeth in a cup,
My eyes on the table until I wake up.
E'er sleep o'ertakes me, I say to myself,
Is there anything else I could lay on the shelf?

The moral of this, as my tale I unfold,
That for you and me who are growing old,
It's better to say, 'I'm fine' with a grin,
Than to let folks know the shape that we're in.

Author unknown

Memories

We met and married a long time ago,
We worked long hours when wages were low.
No TV, no wireless, no bath, times were hard,
Just a cold water tap and a walk in the yard.
No holidays abroad, no carpets on floors,
We had coke on the fire and didn't lock doors.
Our children arrived, no pill in those days,
And we brought them up without state aid.
They were safe going out and played in the park,
Old folk could go for a walk in the dark.
No valium, no drugs, no LSD,
We cured most of our ills with a good cup of tea.
No vandals, no muggings, we had nothing to rob,
We thought we were rich with a couple of bob.
People seemed happier in those far off days,
Kinder and caring in so many ways.
Milkmen and paper-boys would whistle and sing,

A night at the pictures was our one mad fling.
We all had our share of trouble and strife,
We just had to face it, that's the pattern of life.
Now I'm alone I look back through the years,
I don't think of the bad times, the trouble and tears.
I remember our blessings, our home and our love,
And that we shared them together,
I thank God above.

Author unknown

I am old . . . I am like a man on a sea voyage nearing his destination. When I embarked I worried about having a cabin with a porthole, whether I should be asked to sit at the Captain's table, who were the more attractive and important passengers. All such considerations become pointless when I shall so soon be disembarking. As I do not believe that earthly life can bring any lasting satisfaction, the prospect of death holds no terrors. Those saints who pronounced themselves in love with death displayed, I consider, the best of sense.

Malcolm Muggeridge (1903–90)

The unknown shore
Sometime at eve when the tide is low,
I shall slip my mooring and sail away,
With no response to the friendly hail
Of kindred craft in the busy bay.
In the quiet hush of the twilight pale,
When the night stoops down to embrace the day,
And the voices call and the waters flow;
Sometime at eve when the tide is low.
I shall slip my mooring and sail away.
Through purple shadows that darkly trail
O'er the ebbing tide of the unknown sea,
I shall fare me away with a dip of sail
And a ripple of water to tell the tale
Of a lonely voyager sailing away
To mystic isles where at anchor lay

The craft of those who have gone before
O'er the unknown sea to the unknown shore.
A few who have watched me sail away
Will miss my craft from the busy bay.
Some loving souls that my heart holds dear,
In silent sorrow will drop a tear,
But I shall have peacefully furled my sail
In moorings sheltered from storm and gale,
And greet family and friends who have gone before
O'er the unknown sea to the unknown shore.

Elizabeth Clark Hardy (1849–1929)

Classical and traditional

Footprints in the sand
One night I dreamed I was walking
along the beach with the Lord,

many scenes from my life flashed across the sky.
In each scene I noticed footprints in the sand.

Sometimes there were two sets of footprints.
Other times there was only one.

This bothered me because I noticed
during the low periods of my life when I was

suffering from anguish, sorrow or defeat,
I could only see one set of footprints.

So I said to the Lord, 'You promised me,
Lord, that if I followed You,
You would walk with me always.

But I noticed during the most trying periods
of my life there has only been
one set of prints in the sand.

Why, when I needed You most,
have you not been there for me?'

The Lord replied,
'The times when you have seen only one set of footprints
it was then that I carried you.'

Author unknown

Remember

Remember me when I am gone away,
Gone far away into the silent land;
When you can no more hold me by the hand,
Nor I half turn to go, yet turning stay.
Remember me when no more, day by day,
You tell me of our future that you planned:
Only remember me; you understand
It will be late to counsel then or pray.
Yet if you should forget me for a while
And afterwards remember, do not grieve:
For if the darkness and corruption leave
A vestige of the thoughts that I once had,
Better by far you should forget and smile
Than that you should remember and be sad.

Christina Georgina Rossetti (1830–94)

Death is nothing at all

Death is nothing at all. I have only slipped away into the next room. I am I, and you are you. Whatever we were to each other, that we still are. Call me by my old familiar name, speak to me in the easy way that you always used. Put no difference in your tone, wear no forced air of solemnity or sorrow. Laugh as we always laughed at the little jokes we enjoyed together. Play, smile, think of me, pray for me. Let my name be ever the household word that it always was; let it be spoken without effect, without the trace of a shadow on it.

Life means all that it ever meant. It is the same as it ever was; there is unbroken continuity. Why should I be out of mind because I am out of sight? I am waiting for you, for an interval, somewhere very near, just around the corner.

All is well.

Henry Scott Holland (1847–1918)
from 'Grant us thy light', vv. 4–5 (altered)

Death be not proud

Death be not proud, though some have called thee
Mighty and dreadful, for, thou art not so,
For, those, whom thou thinkst, thou dost overthrow,
Die not, poor death, nor yet canst thou kill me.
From rest and sleep, which but thy pictures be,
Much pleasure, then from thee, much more must flow,
And soonest our best men with thee do go,
Rest of their bones, and soul's delivery.
Thou art slave to Fate, Chance, kings and desperate men,
And dost with poison, war, and sickness dwell,
And poppy, or charms can make us sleep as well,
And better than thy stroke: why swell'st thou then?
One short sleep past, we wake eternally,
And death shall be no more; death, thou shalt die.

John Donne (1572–1631), Holy Sonnets, x, xiii

Non-religious

Funeral blues

Stop all the clocks, cut off the telephone,
Prevent the dog from barking with a juicy bone,
Silence the pianos and with muffled drum
Bring out the coffin, let the mourners come.

Let aeroplanes circle moaning overhead
Scribbling on the sky the message He is Dead,
Put crêpe bows round the necks of the public doves,
Let the traffic policemen wear black cotton gloves.

He was my North, my South, my East and West,
My working week and my Sunday rest,
My noon, my midnight, my talk, my song;
I thought that love would last for ever: I was wrong.

The stars are not wanted now; put out every one;
Pack up the moon and dismantle the sun;

Pour away the ocean and sweep up the wood;
For nothing now can ever come to any good.

W. H. Auden (1907–73)

Do not stand at my grave and weep
Do not stand at my grave and weep;
I am not there. I do not sleep.
I am a thousand winds that blow.
I am the diamond glints on snow.
I am the sunlight on ripened grain.
I am the gentle autumn rain.

When you awaken in the morning's hush
I am the swift uplifting rush
Of quiet birds in circled flight.
I am the soft stars that shine at night.
Do not stand at my grave and cry;
I am not there. I did not die.

Mary Elizabeth Frye (1905–2004)

I'm here for a short visit only
I'm here for a short visit only
And I'd rather be loved than hated
Eternity may be lonely
When my body's disintegrated
And that which is loosely termed my soul
Goes whizzing off through the infinite
By means of some vague remote control
I'd like to think I was missed a bit.

Noël Coward (1899–1973)

Farewell my friends
It was beautiful
As long as it lasted
The journey of my life.
I have no regrets
Whatsoever, save
The pain I'll leave behind.

Those dear hearts
Who love and care . . .
And the strings pulling
At the heart and soul . . .

The strong arms
That held me up
When my own strength
Let me down.

At every turning of my life
I came across
Good friends,
Friends who stood by me
Even when the time raced by.

Farewell, farewell
My friends,
I smile and
Bid you goodbye.
No, shed no tears,
For I need them not,
All I need is your smile.

If you feel sad,
Do think of me
For that's what I'll like.
When you live in the hearts
Of those you love,
Remember then,
You never die.

Rabindranath Tagore (1861–1941)

Remember me
To the living I am gone
To the sorrowful I will never return
To the angry I was cheated
But to the happy, I am at peace

And to the faithful, I have never left.
I cannot speak, but I can listen
I cannot be seen, but I can be heard
So as you stand upon the shore
Gazing at the beautiful sea, remember me
As you look in awe at a mighty forest
And its grand majesty, remember me
Remember me in your hearts,
In your thoughts, and the memories of the
Times we loved, and the times we cried, the
Battle we fought and the times we laughed
For if you always think of me, I will
Have never gone.

Author unknown

Because he lived
Because he lived, next door a child
To see him coming, often smiled,
And thought him her devoted friend
Who gladly gave her coins to spend.

Because he lived, a neighbour knew
A clump of tall delphiniums blue
And oriental poppies red
He'd given for a flower bed.

Because he lived, a man in need
Was grateful for a kindly deed
And ever after tried to be
As thoughtful and as fine as he.

Because he lived, ne'er great or proud
Or known to all the motley crowd,
A few there were whose tents were pitched
Near his who found their lives enriched.

Edgar A. Guest (1881–1959)

The life that I have
Is all that I have
And the life that I have is yours.

The love that I have
Of the life that I have
Is yours and yours and yours.

A sleep I shall have
A rest I shall have
Yet death will be but a pause

For the peace of my years
In the long green grass
Will be yours and yours and yours.

Author unknown

So many different lengths of time
How long is a man's life, finally?
Is it a thousand days, or only one?
One week, or a few centuries?
How long does a man's death last?
And what do we mean when we say, 'gone forever'?

Adrift in such preoccupations, we seek clarification.
We can go to the philosophers,
But they will grow tired of our questions.
We can go to the priests and the rabbis,
But they might be too busy with administrations.

So, how long does a man live, finally?
And how much does he live while he lives?
We fret, and ask so many questions –
Then when it comes to us
The answer is so simple.

A man lives for as long as we carry him inside us
For as long as we carry the harvest of his dreams,
For as long as we ourselves live,
Holding memories in common, a man lives.

His lover will carry his man's scent, his touch;
His children will carry the weight of his love.
One friend will carry his arguments,
Another will hum his favourite tunes,
Another will still share his terrors.

And the days will pass with baffled faces,
Then the weeks, then the months,
Then there will be a day when no question is asked,
And the knots of grief will loosen in the stomach,
And the puffed faces will calm.
And on that day he will not have ceased,
But will have ceased to be separated by death.
How long does a man live finally?

A man lives so many different lengths of time.

Brian Patten

'don't tell me that I mourn too much'
don't tell me that I mourn too much
and I won't tell you that you mourn too much
don't tell me that I mourn too little
and I won't tell you that you mourn too little
don't tell me that I mourn in the wrong place
and I won't tell you that you mourn in the wrong place
don't tell me that I mourn at the wrong time
and I won't tell you that you mourn at the wrong time
don't tell me that I mourn in the wrong way
and I won't tell you that you mourn in the wrong way

I may get it wrong, I will get it wrong, I have got it wrong
but don't tell me

Michael Rosen

The suicides
It is hard for us to enter
the kind of despair they must have known
and because it is hard we must get in by breaking
the lock if necessary for we have not the key,
though for them there was no lock and the surrounding walls

were supple, receiving as waves, and they drowned
though not lovingly; it is we only
who must enter in this way.

Temptations will beset us, once we are in.
We may want to catalogue what they have stolen.
We may feel suspicion; we may even criticise the décor
of their suicidal despair, may perhaps feel
it was incongruously comfortable.
Knowing the temptations then
let us go in
deep to their despair and their skin and know
they died because words they had spoken
returned always homeless to them.

Janet Frame

Suicide in the trenches

I knew a simple soldier boy
Who grinned at life in empty joy,
Slept soundly through the lonesome dark,
And whistled early with the lark.

In winter trenches, cowed and glum,
With crumps and lice and lack of rum,
He put a bullet through his brain.
No one spoke of him again.

You smug-faced crowds with kindling eye
Who cheer when soldier lads march by,
Sneak home and pray you'll never know
The hell where youth and laughter go.

Siegfried Sassoon (1886–1967)

8

Additional prayers

———•◆•———

For the death of a child

> Most loving God,
> losing a child is devastating.
> Bless all women,
> and especially _____,
> who have had a miscarriage.
> Comfort them in their loss.
> Give them hope
> for children to come.
> Bless them with an abundance of love
> that as their bodies heal, so too may their hearts.
> Give them courage to face each new day
> in the confidence of your love;
> in the name of Jesus Christ we pray.
>
> *Vienna Cobb Anderson*

Lord, this dreadful thing has happened, and our minds are baffled, our spirits weighed down with grief.

It is beyond our understanding why this little life should be taken, or why we should be called upon to suffer so terrible a loss.

Yet we know that life is full of mystery and that many others at this time are facing the same problem and enduring the same anguish as ourselves.

Help us to bear our sorrow without bitterness, and not to question your love; for to whom can we look for comfort but to you, O Lord?

Speak your word of peace to our hearts; ease our pain and lift our darkness; and be to us a very present help in trouble; for Jesus Christ's sake.

Frank Colquhoun

God our Creator,
from whom all life comes,
comfort this family,
grieving for the loss of their hoped-for child.
Help them to find assurance
that with you nothing is wasted or incomplete,
and uphold them with your love,
through Jesus Christ our Saviour.

A New Zealand Prayer Book

Father of all, stretch out your loving arms to the mother and father who mourn their child,_____ . Draw them gently to you in their grief; comfort them in the emptiness that is left, and give them strength and courage to face the future.

Lord, give us understanding and compassion to say the right words and be sensitive to their needs.

Eunice Davies

The following prayers were prepared by members of the Joint Liturgical Group (an ecumenical creative worship group, offering rites and texts to churches and ecumenical bodies).

The death of a child

We had so many hopes, so many fears,
there has been so much joy, so much sorrow,
and now all our words seem empty.
What we want we cannot have;
and what we thought was promised
has been taken from us.

Silence.

O God,
do not let our pain turn to bitterness
that devours us and kills us.
We thank you for all that is good.
Help us to find peace in troubled times,
and light in our darkness.
These things we ask through Jesus Christ our Lord. **Amen**.

JLG

The death of a son or daughter

Father God,
who watched your own Son die,
our hearts ache beyond our describing –
they break and we feel beyond all comfort.
The heavens seem shut,
and the earth is a wilderness of sorrow and grief.
With your Son on his cross we cry,
'My God, my God, why have you abandoned me?'

Silence.

JLG

For one who has died full of years

Eternal God,
you are from everlasting to everlasting
and your love is on all you have made.

We thank you for *N* _____,
for the years you gave *her*
and the years we shared with *her*.

Here on earth you gave *her* length of days,
grant to *her* now the grace of forgiveness
and the gift of life everlasting.

These things we ask through Jesus Christ, your Son,
who lives and reigns with you in unity of the Holy Spirit,
now and for ever. **Amen**.

JLG

Where faith is difficult

We scarcely know the words to speak,
We scarcely know if they are heard.
When all seems dark, we look for light,
When all is pain, we long for help.
In the silence we wait.

Silence.

We grieve for *N* and mourn our loss.
Accept all that was good in *her*.
Forgive all that was wrong in *her* and in us.
For past joy we give thanks,
In present sorrow we seek courage.
In the silence we wait.

Silence.

JLG

A murder victim

O God we are angry,
we have been robbed of *N*,
and *she* has been robbed of life.
We have wept
till there were no tears left to shed;
and still we weep.
We have shouted,
we have called to you.
Yet our voice returns empty
and the heavens seem deaf to our cry.
Your Son died a victim too.
O God, we are weeping with you.

Silence.

JLG

The victim of an accident

O God, why *N*?
We long for an answer,
but no answer is good enough.
She is gone,
and we are left with questions.
Grant us courage to leave *her* with you.
O God, we want to believe.
Help us where faith runs out.
This we ask through Jesus Christ your Son. **Amen**.

JLG

One who has died suddenly

O God, we are stunned.

We cannot take it in.
It sees unreal and yet all too real.
Save us from simply blaming ourselves and others;
bear with us the pain and guilt of what has happened;
and give us the healing
of wounds that now run deep.
We make our prayers through Jesus Christ our Lord. **Amen**.

God of all time,
this time seems wrong, too soon.
Help us to believe that this time and all times
are your time.
On this day of grief
speak your word of resurrection,
that with *N* we may hear your voice and live.
This we ask through Jesus Christ our Lord. **Amen**.

JLG

One who has died after a long illness

God of all the years,
you hold the keys of life and death.
For *N* the journey has been slow and hard,

the days of illness long and wearisome.
Lead *her* home now to you,
that *she* may rest where pain and agony are no more
and where you wipe away all tears.
Be *her* eternal light,
and grant *her* to eat from the tree of life:
these things we ask through Jesus Christ our Lord. **Amen**.

JLG

One who has died after a dementia or similar condition

Loving God,
we have seen this day from afar.
For so many days *N* has seemed remote from us,
and we have lost *her* as she seemed to lose us.
Yet you have known us all,
and you have kept us with *her* in your eternal love.
Welcome home the one we mourn,
the friend who became a stranger.
Grant to *her* the recognition of your face
and that life which never fades.
These things we ask through Jesus Christ,
your Son, our Lord. **Amen**.

JLG

One who has died after surgery

Our loss is heavy, our pain is fierce and deep;
we had hoped that *N* would live.
and now we remember how fragile life is,
how hard others fought to save the one we loved.
Grant that what can be turned to good will be,
and that what we cannot call back we may let go.
God of life and death,
we deliver into your care our friend [and *mother/father* . . .].
Bring *her* into the company of your saints
who dwell in light and life eternal;
through Jesus Christ our Lord. **Amen**.

JLG

One who has died in loneliness

God of the homeless, the widow and the orphan,
remember *N*, whom so many ignored or forgot,
and grant to *her* and all like *her*
a home and shelter in your love,
for you treasure all that you have made.
Gather *her* and greet *her* with gentleness,
so that *she* may find at last true dignity and worth
as *she* is transformed to reveal the image of your Son,
Jesus Christ, who lived and died with the outcast and the stranger.

Hear us as we make our prayer in his name,
who lives for ever with you in the unity of the Holy Spirit,
One God for ever and ever. **Amen.**

JLG

After long-term care

We thank you, our God,
for those who have cared for *N*
in these last days [over many days].
We remember their skill and their kindness,
we recall their watchful eye, their soothing hand.
We thank you for those
who brought relief from pain,
and shared our burden with us.
Accept our thanks, our God,
and make us ready to give as we have received;
through Jesus Christ our Lord. **Amen.**

JLG

Following a natural disaster

Where, O God, were you?
Did you not care?
Have you hidden from us all hope and believing?

Our hearts and minds reel,
our thoughts and speech outrun reason
and we cry out in pain.

O God, where are you?
Do not hide your face from us.
Do not leave us without comfort or solace.

When we run to the ends of the earth,
when we rage in the dark of the night,
meet us there
and grant us peace, and hope enough
to entrust *N* to you.
With all who suffer today we cry to you.

Lord, in your mercy,
Hear our prayer.

JLG

Following a disaster arising from human error or accident

Suddenly, O God,
we have lost *the one/those* we love.
In hurt, in anger, in despair,
meet us where we are.

We long for answers,
to learn and put right what we can.
May the truth set us free.

Give us courage to bear what cannot be undone.
Comfort us and all who mourn with us.

For *N and all who have suffered*
We make our prayers.
Bring *them* by your mercy to that place where suffering is no more.
This we ask through Jesus Christ, your Son, our Lord. **Amen.**

JLG

For general use

Loving God,
we are lost and it is dark;
we are hurt, but we feel nothing;
we know, yet we cannot take it in.

Give light to our footsteps,
heal our wounds,
and lead us to your truth:
Jesus Christ, who died but now is arisen. **Amen.**

JLG

O Comforting One,
Compassionate One,
be with us all
when we suffer loss
and ache with the pain of grieving.
Give us a glimpse
of the way it will be
when love will never be taken away,
when life itself will not be diminished,
when all that we hold most precious
will live and remain with us for ever.

Miriam Therese Winter

A suicide

It is too hard to bear,
N's pain was more than *she* could stand;
and now we suffer pain – not *hers* but ours.
O God, *N* saw no other way out,
lead *her* now to Christ who bore his pain to death,
and grant *her* peace.
This we ask though Jesus Christ our Lord. **Amen.**

JLG

O God righteous and compassionate,
forgive the despair of _____ for whom we pray.
Heal in *him/her* that which is broken,
and in your great love stand with those
hurt by the violence of *his/her* end.
Lord be to *him/her* not a judge but a Saviour.
Receive *him/her* into that kingdom wherein by your mercy
we sinners also would have place,

Through the merits of our wounded Redeemer
Who lives and reigns with you in the Holy Spirit's power
Now and unto the ages of ages.

Elizabeth Basset (slightly adapted)

Lord Jesus,
as you bowed your head and died,
a great darkness covered the land.

We lay before you
the despair of all
who find life
without meaning or purpose,
and see no value in themselves,
who suffer the anguish
of inner darkness
that can only lead them
to self-destruction and death.

Lord,
in your passion, you too
felt abandoned, isolated, derelict.

You are one
with all who suffer
pain and torment
of body and mind.

Be to them the light
that has never been mastered.
Pierce the darkness
which surrounds and engulfs them,
so that they may know
within themselves
acceptance, forgiveness, and peace.

We pray for those who,
through the suicide of one close to them,
suffer the emptiness of loss
and the burden of untold guilt.
May they know your gift of acceptance,

so that they may be freed
from self-reproach
and mutual recrimination,
and find in the pattern
of your dying and rising,
new understanding, and purpose
for their lives.

Neville Smith

The gift of tears
Lord, we give you thanks for the gift of tears:
For tears of grief, redeeming our mourning from despair;
For tears of anger, awakening our thirst for justice;
For tears of laughter, celebrating our joy in living.

May the light of Christ shining through our tears
Become the rainbow of your promise,
Shedding colours of your love's bright presence
In your grieving, struggling, laughing world.

Author unknown

God of all consolation,
In your unending love and mercy for us.
You turn the darkness of death
Into the dawn of new life.
Show compassion to your people in their sorrow.

Be our refuge and our strength
To lift us from the darkness of this grief
To the peace and light of your presence.

Your son, our Lord Jesus Christ,
By dying for us, conquered death
And by rising again, restored life.

May we then go forward eagerly to meet him,
And after our life on earth
Be reunited with our brothers and sisters
Where every tear will be wiped away.

Author unknown

Grant, O Lord, to all who are bereaved, the spirit of faith and courage, that they may have the strength to meet the days to come with steadfastness and patience; not sorrowing as those without hope, but in thankful remembrance of thy great goodness in past years, and in the sure expectation of a joyful reunion in the heavenly places; and this we ask in the name of Jesus Christ our Lord.

Church of Ireland, Book of Common Prayer

O God, who brought us to birth
and in whose arms we die:
in our grief and shock
contain and comfort us,
embrace us with your love,
give us hope in our confusion
and grace to let go into new life;
through Jesus Christ, **Amen.**

Janet Morley

Lord, make us instruments of your peace.
Where there is hatred, let us sow love;
Where there is injury, pardon;
Where there is discord, union;
Where there is doubt, faith;
Where there is despair, hope;
Where there is darkness, light;
Where there is sadness, joy;
O divine master, grant that we may not so much seek
To be consoled as to console,
To be understood as to understand,
To be loved as to love.
For it is in giving that we receive;
It is in pardoning that we are pardoned;
And it is in dying that we are born to eternal life.
Amen.

Attributed to St Francis of Assisi (1181–1226) (adapted)

We remember, Lord, the slenderness of the thread which separates life from death, and the suddenness with which it can be broken. Help us also to remember that on both sides of that division we are surrounded by your love.

Persuade our hearts that when our dear ones die neither we nor they are parted from you.

In you may we find peace, and in you be united with them in the body of Christ, who has burst the bonds of death and is alive for evermore, our Saviour and theirs for ever and ever.

Dick Williams

A simple but effective way of combining family participation with prayer involves placing four candles at the front of the church. At the appropriate time, the minister invites four family members or friends to come forward one at a time to light a candle and to read the following words:

The first candle represents our grief.
The pain of losing you is intense.
It reminds us of the depth of our love for you.

The second candle represents our courage.
To confront our sorrow,
To comfort each other,
To change our lives.

The third candle we light in your memory.
For the times we laughed,
The times we cried,
The times we were angry with each other,
The silly things you did,
The caring and joy you gave us.

The fourth candle we light for our love.
We light this candle that your light will always shine
As we enter this sad time and share this day of remembrance
With family and friends.
We cherish the special place in our hearts
That will always be reserved for you.

We thank you for the gift
Your living brought to each of us.

Author unknown

This is a personal prayer written by the family of Hilda, whose funeral is referred to in Chapter 1. It is included in the hope that its simplicity might encourage others to write a similar prayer on behalf of their own loved one.

We thank God for Hilda's long life,
  not without its troubles,
  but with a core of love and faith enabling her to carry on.
For her happy childhood and loving home.
For her contented marriage and satisfaction in her home and
  children.
For surviving two world wars without losing any close family.
For her caring role as a mother and then as a teacher,
  bringing the best out of difficult pupils.
For her wish to encourage others and be helpful.
For the support she received in her own bereavement, which hit
  her very hard.
For her courage in moving North at the age of 74, starting a new
  life with new people and activities.
For her widening horizons in old age, meeting a variety of
  people and campaigning against world poverty.
For the great encouragement she received from others, helping
  her through loneliness and then through anxiety and fear
  caused by her loss of memory from the age of 90.
For her ability to accept graciously the care she needed from
  professional carers at home, in residential care and in
  hospital.
For her feeling of safety at last, safe with others and safe in the
  hands of God.

Chris and Mike Cresswell

The serenity prayer
God, give us grace to accept with serenity
the things that cannot be changed,
courage to change the things that should be changed,
and the wisdom to distinguish the one from the other.

Reinhold Niebuhr (1892–1971)

A Celtic blessing
Deep peace of the running wave to you,
Deep peace of the flowing air to you,
Deep peace of the quiet earth to you,
Deep peace of the shining stars to you,
Deep peace of the Son of Peace to you.
May the road rise to meet you;
May the wind be always at your back;
May the sun shine warm upon your face;
May the rains fall softly upon your fields,
Until we meet again,
May God hold you in the hollow of His hand.

Author unknown

Support us, O Lord, all the day long,
Until the shadows lengthen, the evening comes,
The busy world is hushed,
The fever of life is over and our work done.
Then, in your mercy, grant us a safe lodging,
A holy rest, and peace at the last;
Through Jesus Christ our Lord. **Amen**.

Cardinal John Henry Newman (1801–1890)

9

Music, hymns and songs

------◆◆◆------

Popular modern music that can be played before, during or after the service

A day without rain – Enya
Affirmation – Savage Garden
Akuna Matata (from *The Lion King*) – Elton John
All that matters – Cliff Richard
Angel – Sarah McLachlan
Angels – Robbie Williams
Angels among us – Alabama
Annie's song – John Denver
Amazing grace – Michael Crawford
Beautiful day – U2
Because you loved me – Celine Dion
Blowing in the wind – Bob Dylan
Bridge over troubled waters – Simon and Garfunkel
Can you feel the love tonight? (from *The Lion King*) – Elton John
Candle in the wind – Elton John
Children – Robert Miles
Circle of life – Elton John
Death is not the end – Bob Dylan
Don't look back in anger – Oasis
Don't wanna lose you – Gloria Estefan
Everybody hurts – REM
Fields of gold – Eva Cassidy
Fly – Celine Dion
Forever young – Bob Dylan
Funeral for a friend – Elton John
Gone too soon – Michael Jackson

He ain't heavy, he's my brother – The Hollies
Hero – Mariah Carey
Hey now, hey now – Crowded House
If tomorrow never comes – Ronan Keating
If you love somebody (set them free) – Sting
I need a hero – Bonnie Tyler
I will always love you – Whitney Houston
I will remember you – Sarah McLachlan
I'll be missing you – Puff Daddy, Faith Evans and 112
I'll fly away – Aretha Franklin
In my life – The Beatles
Lady in red – Chris De Burgh
Looking through your eyes – Leann Rimes
Love is a beautiful thing – Tina Turner
Love me tender – Elvis Presley
Make me a channel of your peace – Sinead O'Connor
Mama – Il Divo
May it be – Enya
Memories – Barbara Streisand
Memories – Elvis Presley
Millennium (Lord's) Prayer – Cliff Richard
Missing you – Diana Ross
Morning has broken – Cat Stevens
Music box – Mariah Carey
My heart will go on – Celine Dion
My way – Frank Sinatra
Never tear us apart – INXS
Nothing compares 2U – Sinead O'Connor
November rain – Guns 'n Roses
Oceans – Pearl Jam
One day at a time – Patty Newton
One moment in time – Whitney Houston
One of us – Abba
One sweet day – Mariah Carey and Boys II Men
Only time – Enya
Pie Jesu – John Rutter
Portrait of my love – Matt Monro
Prayer – Celine Dion

Save a prayer – Duran Duran
Simply the best – Tina Turner
Somewhere over the rainbow – Eva Cassidy
Songbird – Eva Cassidy
Stairway to heaven – Led Zeppelin
Tears in heaven – Eric Clapton
The day you went away – Wendy Matthews
The living years – Mike and the Mechanics
The long and winding road – Beatles
The Lord bless you and keep you – John Rutter
The Lord's my shepherd – John Rutter
The rose – Bette Midler
There you'll be – Faith Hill
Time to say goodbye – Sarah Brightman
To where you are – G4
Unchained melody – Elvis Presley
Unforgettable – Nat King Cole
Watermark – Enya
We'll meet again – Vera Lynn
What a wonderful world – Louis Armstrong
When I fall in love – Nat King Cole
When you say nothing at all – Ronan Keating
Who wants to live forever? – Queen
Wind beneath my wings – Bette Midler
Wings of a dove – Charley Pride
Wish you were here – Bee Gees
You have been loved – George Michael
You were loved – Whitney Houston
You'll never walk alone – Gerry and the Pacemakers
You're beautiful – James Blunt

Hymns

Abide with me
All people that on earth do dwell
All things bright and beautiful
Amazing grace

And did those feet (Jerusalem)
Ave Maria
Be not afraid
Be thou my vision
City of God
Dear Lord and Father of mankind
Do not be afraid
Eternal Father, strong to save
For all the saints
For the beauty of the earth
God be in my head
God be with you till we meet again
Great is thy faithfulness
Guide me, O thou great Jehovah
He who would valiant be
Here I am Lord (I the Lord of sea and sky)
How great thou art (O Lord, my God)
How sweet the name of Jesus sounds
I heard the voice of Jesus say
I know that my Redeemer lives
I need thee every hour
I the Lord of sea and sky (Here I am, Lord)
I vow to thee my country
I watch the sunrise
Immortal, invisible, God only wise
In heavenly love abiding
Jerusalem (And did those feet)
Lead us heavenly Father
Lord of all hopefulness
Lord, the light of your love (Shine, Jesus, shine)
Love divine, all loves excelling
Make me a channel of your peace
Mine eyes have seen the glory
Morning has broken
My song is love unknown
Nearer my God to Thee
Now thank we all our God
O God, our help in ages past

O love that wilt not let me go
O Lord, my God (How great thou art)
O praise ye the Lord
O sacred head
On a hill far away (The old rugged cross)
On eagles' wings
Onward Christian soldiers
Panis angelicus
Praise my soul
Praise to the Lord
Rock of ages cleft for me
Shine, Jesus, shine (Lord, the light of your love)
Steal away to Jesus
The day thou gavest Lord is ended
The king of love my shepherd is
The Lord's my shepherd
The old rugged cross (On a hill far away)
There is a green hill far away
There's a wideness in God's mercy
Thine be the glory
What a Friend we have in Jesus
When I survey the wondrous cross

Music for playing on organ or CD at the beginning or end of the service

Albinoni – Adagio in C minor
Allegri – *Miserere mei, Deus*
Bach, J. S. – Air on a G string
Bach, J. S. – Double Violin Concerto in D minor, 2nd movement
Bach, J. S. – Fantasia in C minor
Bach, J. S. – Jesu, joy of man's desiring
Bach, J. S. – Liebster Jesu
Bach, J. S. – Passion Chorale
Bach, J. S. – Sheep may safely graze
Barber – Violin Concerto, 2nd movement
Beethoven – Piano Sonata no. 8 in C major (*Pathétique*), 2nd movement
Beethoven – Piano Sonata no. 14 in C sharp minor ('Moonlight')

Brahms – Lullaby
Brahms – Violin Concerto in D major, 2nd movement
Bruch – Violin Concerto no. 1
Dvořák – Symphony no. 9 in E minor ('New World')
Elgar – Nimrod (*Variations on an Original Theme (Enigma)*)
Fauré – Pavane for Orchestra and Choir Op. 50
Fauré – Pie Jesu (*Requiem*)
Franck – Panis Angelicus
Grieg – Morning (*Peer Gynt*)
Jenkins, Karl – Benedictus (*The Armed Man*)
Handel – Hallelujah Chorus (*The Messiah*)
Handel – I know that my Redeemer liveth (*The Messiah*)
Handel – Largo (*Xerxes*)
Mascagni – Intermezzo (*Cavalleria Rusticana*)
Mendelssohn – Sonata no. 2 in C minor
Mendelssohn – Violin Concerto in E minor, 2nd movement
Mozart – *Ave Verum Corpus*
Mozart – Clarinet concerto in A
Mozart – Piano concerto no. 21 in C
Pachelbel – Canon in D
Parry – Elegy in A flat
Rachmaninov – Piano concerto no. 2 in C minor
Stanford – Postlude in D minor
Thalben-Ball – Elegy no. 2
Vaughan Williams – Prelude on 'Rhosymedre'
Vaughan Williams – *The Lark Ascending*
Walford Davies – *Solemn Melody*

Sources and acknowledgements

I am grateful to a number of people who have inspired and encouraged me to write this book: Dr Tony Walter, whose book *Funerals and How to Improve Them* (Hodder & Stoughton, 1990) first made me think seriously about creating funerals that were appropriate for different people and situations; my colleague and friend Christine Gillespie, who made some valuable contributions to the chapter on the death of a child; the many hundreds of families that have allowed me to share with them in the most poignant moments of their grief and have given me items included in this book; and my wife Kathryn, who has kept our home and family together while I have been sitting for hours in blissful isolation at my desk.

The material contained in this book has been compiled over a period of many years and initially without any intention of producing a book. The consequence of this protracted process is that the identity of some of the sources cannot now be recalled or traced. Every effort has been made to trace the copyright holders of material quoted here. I would like to apologize to any writers who may recognize in this book phrases, ideas and images as their own, and for which I have been unable to ask permission or seek consent for their inclusion. Information on any omissions should be sent to the publisher, who will make full acknowledgement in any future edition.

Rosemary Arthur, full source unknown.

Vienna Cobb Anderson, 'Most loving God' from *Prayers of Our Hearts: In Word and Action* (Crossroad, 1994).

W. H. Auden, 'Funeral Blues' from *Collected Poems* (Faber and Faber, 1976). Copyright © 1936 by W. H. Auden. Reprinted by permission of Curtis Brown Ltd.

Elizabeth Basset, 'O God righteous and compassionate' from *Interpreted by Love: An Anthology of Praise*, ed. Elizabeth Basset (Darton, Longman and Todd, 1994).

Simon Bridges, 'Tomorrows' from *Poems and Readings for Funerals*, ed. Julia Watson (Penguin, 2004). Copyright © 2004 Simon Bridges. Reprinted by kind permission of Jonathan Clowes Ltd, London, on behalf of Julia Watson.

Derek Browning, full source unknown.

Raymond Carver, 'No need' from *All of Us: Collected Poems* (Harvill Press, 1996), copyright © 1996 Tess Gallagher.

Charles Causley, 'Eden Rock' from *Collected Poems 1951–2000* (Macmillan, 2000), reproduced by permission of David Higham Associates Ltd.

Church of Ireland, 'Grant, O Lord, to all who are bereaved' from the Church of Ireland Book of Common Prayer. Reproduced by kind permission of the Church of Ireland.

Frank Colquhoun, 'Lord, this dreadful thing has happened' from *Contemporary Parish Prayers* (Hodder and Stoughton, 1999).

Noël Coward, 'I'm here for a short visit only' from *Collected Verse* (Methuen Publishing, 1984). Copyright © the estate of Noël Coward. Reprinted by permission of Methuen Publishing Ltd.

Chris and Mike Cresswell, 'A prayer for Hilda', reproduced by kind permission of the authors.

Eunice Davies, 'Father of all, stretch out your loving arms' taken from *Women at Prayer: An Anthology of Prayers by Mothers' Union Members from around the World* by Rachel Stowe. Copyright © 1994. Used by permission of The Zondervan Corporation.

Jane Davies, extract from *The Price of Loving* (Mowbray, 1981).

C. Day Lewis, extract from 'A time to dance' in *The Complete Poems of C. Day Lewis* published by Sinclair-Stevenson (1992) in this edition The Estate of C. Day Lewis. Reprinted by permission of The Random House Group Ltd.

ECUSA Book of Common Prayer, 'Father of all, we pray for those whom we love' from the Episcopal Church of the United States of America Book of Common Prayer.

Susan Erling, full source unknown.

Vicki Feaver, 'Coat' from *Close Relatives* (Secker, 1981). Reprinted by kind permission of the author.

Janet Frame, 'The Suicides' from *The Pocket Mirror* (The Women's Press, 1992). Reprinted by permission of the Janet Frame Literary Trust.

Mary Elizabeth Frye, 'Do not stand at my grave and weep' was written in 1932 and is so commonly used that it is considered to be in the public domain.

Fred Pratt Green, 'Lord Jesus, take this child', © 1990 Stainer & Bell Ltd. Reproduced by permission.

Grahame Greene, *The Comedians* (Bodley Head, 1966).

Joyce Grenfell, 'If I should go before the rest of you' (copyright © The Joyce Grenfell Memorial Trust, 1980) is reproduced by permission of Sheil Land Assoicates Ltd on behalf of the estate of Joyce Grenfell.

Edgar A. Guest, 'Because he lived' from *The Collected Verse of Edgar A. Guest* (NTC/Contemporary Publishing Group, Lincolnwood, Ill., 1984).

Christopher Hawes, 'A likely lad', read at the funeral of the character John Archer in the long-running BBC Radio 4 series *The Archers*.

Vladimír Holan 'Resurrection', trans. George Theiner, from *Do Not Go Gentle*, ed. Neil Astley (Bloodaxe Books, 2003).

Jean Holloway, 'O Father, on your love we call', reprinted by kind permission of the author. This hymn was sung at the memorial service held in Dunblane Cathedral for the 16 children and the teacher from Dunblane Primary School who died in the shooting tragedy of 13 March 1996.

Joint Liturgical Group: the prayers are taken from *Funeral Services of the Christian Churches in England* (SCM-Canterbury Press, 2002).

Patrick Kavanagh, 'In memory of my mother' from *Collected Poems*, ed. Antoinette Quinn (Allen Lane, 2004), by kind permission of the Trustees of the Estate of the late Katherine B. Kavanagh, through the Jonathan Williams Literary Agency.

Brendan Kennelly, 'I see you dancing, Father' from *Familiar Strangers: New and Selected Poems 1960–2004* (Bloodaxe Books, 2004), reproduced by permission.

Elisabeth Kübler Ross, 'Returning', full source unknown.

Norah Leney, 'Deep sobbing' from *In a Lifetime* (JMR Publishing Co., New York, 1975).

Dorothy McRae-McMahon, prayers of committal and blessing from *Liturgies for the Journey of Life* (SPCK, 2000).

Methodist Worship Book, Prayers for Funeral Service © Trustees for Methodist Church Purposes, used by permission of Methodist Publishing House.

Janet Morley, 'O God who brought us to birth' from *The SPCK Book of Christian Prayer* (SPCK, 1995). Reproduced by kind permission of the author.

Malcolm Muggeridge, extract from *Jesus Rediscovered* (Fontana, 1969), page 57. By permission of David Higham Associates Ltd.

A New Zealand Prayer Book, 'God our creator', copyright material taken from *A New Zealand Prayer Book – He Karakia Mihinare o Aotearoa*. Reproduced by kind permission of the Anglican Church in Aotearoa, New Zealand and Polynesia.

Reinhold Niebuhr: the Serenity Prayer has often been attributed to others but without sources. Although similar prayers may have existed, the work seems to be Niebuhr's. He never copyrighted the prayer and many variants have been used.

Alden Nowlan, 'This is what I wanted to sign off with' from *Between Tears and Laughter: Selected Poems* (Bloodaxe Books/House of Anansi Press, 2004), reproduced by permission.

Hugh O'Donnell, 'Light', reproduced by kind permission of the author.

Brian Patten, 'So many different lengths of time', copyright © 1996 Brian Patten. Reproduced by permission of the author, c/o Rogers, Coleridge & White Ltd.

Marjorie Pizer, extract from *To You the Living* (Second Back Row Press, Leura, NSW, Australia, 1981).

Michael Rosen, 'don't tell me that I mourn too much' from *Carrying the Elephant* (Penguin, 2002). Copyright © Michael Rosen 2002. Reproduced by permission of Penguin Books Ltd.

Siegfried Sassoon, 'Suicide in the trenches' from *Collected Poems 1908–1956* (Faber and Faber, 1984), © Siegfried Sassoon by kind permission of Mr George Sassoon.

Marilyn Shawe, full source unknown.

Kathryn Smith, 'Why?', 'The cost of loving' and 'You should be here', reproduced by kind permission of the author.

Neville Smith, 'Lord Jesus, as you bowed your head and died' from *Prayers for People in Hospital* (Oxford University Press, 1994), reproduced by permission.

Arlene Stamy, full source unknown.

Anne Stevenson, 'The minister' from *Poems 1955–2005* (Bloodaxe Books, 2005), reproduced by permission.

Rabindranath Tagore, 'Sesher kavita' ('Farewell my friends') from *Collected Poems and Plays* (Macmillan, 1936); 'The end' from *The Crescent Moon* (Macmillan 1915).

Henry Van Dyke, 'Gone from my sight' is commonly attributed to this nineteenth-century American Presbyterian minister, literary critic and writer.

Glyn and Mandy Walker, 'Letters to Eleanor' from Ray Simpson, *Before We Say Goodbye: Preparing for a Good Death* (HarperCollins, 2001), reproduced by kind permission of the authors.

David L. Weatherford, 'Slow dance' is sometimes attributed to a terminally ill young girl in a New York hospital; full source unknown.

Jeanne Willis, 'Inside our dreams' from *Toffee Pockets* (Bodley Head, 1992). Reprinted by permission of The Random House Group Ltd.

Dick Williams, 'We remember, Lord' from *Prayers for Today's Church* (Falcon Books, 1972).

Miriam Therese Winter, 'O Comforting One' from *Woman Wisdom: A Feminist Lectionary and Psalter: Women of the Hebrew Scriptures, Part One* (Crossroad, 1991).

Mary Yarnell, 'Too soon' from *Poems and Readings for Funerals*, ed. Julia Watson (Penguin, 2004). Copyright © 2004 Mary Yarnell. Reprinted by kind permission of Jonathan Clowes Ltd, London, on behalf of Julia Watson.

Index of Subjects and Authors

The Society for Promoting Christian Knowledge (SPCK) was founded in 1698. Its mission statement is:

To promote Christian knowledge by

- **Communicating the Christian faith in its rich diversity;**
- **Helping people to understand the Christian faith and to develop their personal faith; and**
- **Equipping Christians for mission and ministry.**

SPCK Worldwide serves the Church through Christian literature and communication projects in over 100 countries, and provides books for those training for ministry in many parts of the developing world. This worldwide service depends upon the generosity of others and all gifts are spent wholly on ministry programmes, without deductions.

SPCK Bookshops support the life of the Christian community by making available a full range of Christian literature and other resources, providing support for those training for ministry, and assisting bookstalls and book agents throughout the UK.

SPCK Publishing produces Christian books and resources, covering a wide range of inspirational, pastoral, practical and academic subjects. Authors are drawn from many different Christian traditions, and publications aim to meet the needs of a wide variety of readers in the UK and throughout the world.

The Society does not necessarily endorse the individual views contained in its publications, but hopes they stimulate readers to think about and further develop their Christian faith.

For further information about the Society, visit our website at *www.spck.org.uk* or write to:
SPCK, 36 Causton Street,
London SW1P 4ST, United Kingdom.